FIBERGLASS REPAIR

FIBERGLASS
REPAIR
POLYESTER OR EPOXY

David and Zora Aiken
illustrated by David Aiken

CORNELL MARITIME PRESS
Centreville, Maryland

Library of Congress Cataloging-in-Publication Data

Aiken, Zora.
Fiberglass repair : with polyester or epoxy / Zora and David Aiken ; illustrated
by David Aiken.—1st ed.
    p. cm.
Includes bibliographical references and index.
ISBN-13: 978-0-87033-567-9 (alk. paper)
1. Glass reinforced plastics. 2. Glass fibers. I. Aiken, David, 1940- II. Title.
TA455.P55A32 2005
623.8'458'0288—dc22

                         2005005819

Manufactured in the United States of America
First edition, 2005

To all boatowners who like to say, "I did it myself."

Contents

Preface

Fiberglass repair is often regarded as a job best left to the professionals. True, a fiberglass fix can't be hammered or welded into place, but the perception of difficulty is more likely caused by concern that the products are hard to work with. Boatyard reports of sagging epoxy and uncured gelcoat abound, yet the unheard stories tell a different tale. Hundreds of restored fiberglass boats—twenty, thirty, even forty years old—are still afloat, still providing all the joys of boating, but with the added satisfaction that the owner can point proudly to all kinds of repairs and modifications and say "I did it myself."

Despite the availability of different types of both reinforcements and resins, the general procedures for repair are common to most. We hope this book will encourage boatowners to try their hand at repairs. The savings on labor costs should be welcome, but beyond that, pride of ownership is a nice concept. And the more repairing, restoring, or rebuilding, the more pride.

For technical assistance and advice, we acknowledge and thank the following sources: the original *Fiberglass Repairs* by Paul J. Petrick; manuals and *Epoxyworks* magazine published by Gougeon Brothers, manufacturer of WEST system epoxies; members of Gougeon Brothers technical staff; *The Epoxy Book,* a Systems Three Resins publication; Evercoat, manufacturer of polyester supplies; and 3M, manufacturer of repair and maintenance products as well as safety gear.

We are also grateful to the many boatyard owners and managers who saw us through the maintenance, repair, and restoration of an assortment of fiberglass boats, including our present home, a fiberglass motorsailer that, at age forty, can finally be called a classic instead of an old boat.

Introduction

When fiberglass construction was first introduced to the recreational boat market over fifty years ago, it was impossible to predict its impact on the industry. Would people accept the new material? Were fiberglass boats strong enough to be safe? How long would they last?

The intervening years have shown that the public would indeed accept the "plastic" boats—by the thousands, in all sizes and shapes. Properly constructed, fiberglass boats proved to be remarkably tough and durable. Perhaps best of all, even when damage does occur, most of it can be repaired, even by inexperienced amateurs. Properly maintained, fiberglass boats age gracefully, having already become classics in many categories.

Fiberglass is, of course, only one part of the composite material described as "fiber-reinforced-plastic" (also "fiberglass-reinforced plastic") or FRP. The fiberglass itself is exactly what the word suggests—fine filaments of glass that are woven into a fabric, pressed into a mat, or held together by stitching or an attached backing. Fiberglass becomes boat-building material when used in combination with resin (liquid plastic).

Early fiberglass boats were built in molds by the "hand lay-up" or "solid lay-up" method. Fabric plies were layered into the mold and saturated with resin one by one until the appropriate hull thickness was reached. With this early construction, "appropriate" might be 1½ inches or more—much thicker than necessary as ongoing development would show.

Later, some manufacturers used "chopper gun" technology, whereby small bits of chopped fiberglass strands and resin were simultaneously "shot" into the mold to build the hull thickness.

Eventually, other builders used "sandwich construction" in which a core material was sandwiched between two thin fiberglass skins, gaining the advantage of strength in a lightweight hull.

Today, different types of resin and different types of reinforcing fibers may be used, but the term "fiberglass" remains the generic term to describe the end result of any of the fiber/resin combinations.

Which type of material to use for repairs may be dictated by the original materials or the type of damage. When considering the original construction, however, it must be remembered that all layers of cloth and resin were chemically bonded because the resin cured at essentially the same time; this is called primary bonding. In repair work, the new-to-old bond cannot have the same characteristics as the original and must be mechanical; this is called secondary bonding. When choosing the repair material, it is reasonable to consider that the repair material should be the same as, or better than, the original to ensure adequate secondary bonding.

Experienced fiberglass workers are often called artists, not in the creative sense, but because of their ability to produce the near-perfect finishes expected by builders and owners. It wouldn't hurt the novice do-it-yourselfer to adopt some of that perfectionist attitude, but acceptable repairs can be done by the determined beginner. Careful attention to good instructions, a bit of practice with the materials, and patience can bring a satisfactory result.

Just as with any new procedure, the first-time worker should start with a small project, in order to get a feel for the materials and the tools. Given enough time and inclination, the larger repairs can be approached with a level of confidence. The willingness to attempt more complicated jobs should be significantly bolstered by the knowledge that if the first fix doesn't work, the failure can be removed and the repair done over. The job will be messy and it won't be fun, but fiberglass allows as many tries as it takes.

Once a person is familiar with the properties of fiberglass, it is a source of both surprise and satisfaction to realize how many things besides boats can be repaired with the material. Cars and recreational vehicles of all types come to mind as the most obvious. Add to those a long list of applications in home construction: architectural trim, household plumbing, plaster and concrete patching, and decking repair. Smaller projects include furniture, picture frames, scale models, and musical instruments. In short, the possibilities are limited only by an individual's willingness and ability to improvise.

FIBERGLASS REPAIR

Chapter 1

Materials

Fiberglass fabric and liquid resin are the two components of fiber-glass-reinforced plastic (FRP). For many repairs, the resin is also thickened to a putty-like consistency to use as an adhesive, a filler, or a fairing compound. Various types of thickening agents are used, each intended for a particular purpose. Pigments, solvents, and cleaners complete the basic materials list.

FIBERGLASS

Fiberglass is available in many forms, and while most types will be mentioned and defined in this book, the emphasis will be on those materials used most commonly for typical repairs.

Woven Fabric

Woven fabric is selected for most projects. It's the most economical, and it can be purchased in different weights to suit specific jobs. It is described and priced according to weight, which is stated in a given number of ounces per square yard. Ten-ounce cloth is probably the most popular choice.

Fabric can be purchased in folded sheets (individual pieces or as one component of a repair kit) or in continuous yardage from rolls of cloth in varying widths. It is difficult to keep fiberglass cloth intact in its neatly woven state. Like ordinary fabrics, it is a cross weave of fibers running at 90 degrees to each other. Once cut, the edge fibers want to escape, just like the threads of other fabrics, only seemingly more so. Dealing with the unraveling of cloth is one of the first learned arts of fiberglassing. The cloth can be used in full-fabric-width pieces to cover large areas, or it can be cut into pieces of any size and shape for small jobs.

Tape

Fabric is also made in narrow strips called "tape," which can be purchased in rolls, much like other kinds of tape, or ordered by the yard from the supplier's continuous roll. When a narrow patch is to be made, the tape makes a neat job because its edges are finished or nonraveling. It is handy for covering seams or adding support at chines or other places where extra strength or increased abrasion-resistance is desirable.

Mat

Mat is a style of fabric made of short strands of fiberglass (about an inch long) that are pressed together into a flat, smooth material. Generally thicker than cloth, mat is available in different weights too, from ¾ ounce to 3 ounce (described in ounces per square foot rather than ounces per square yard). For general repair, 1½ ounce is usually chosen.

In the most common type of mat, the chopped strands are held together with a binder. When polyester resin is applied, the binder dissolves, allowing the mat to saturate readily and drape more easily over curved surfaces. At one time, it was thought that mat should not be used with epoxy resin because the binder would not dissolve, but a study by a manufacturer of epoxy products (Gougeon Brothers) concluded that the presence of the binder does not affect the curing nor the strength of the end product, good news for those who like to work with mat. Though mat is not as strong as woven fabric, it has the distinct advantage of building up a thickness quicker. When laminating a hull or deck patch, the standard recommendation is to alternate layers of cloth and mat.

Woven Roving

For an extremely fast buildup of thickness, woven roving was the only choice for years. Used in the initial construction of most fiberglass boats, this is a heavy-weight, loosely woven fabric made of large strands of glass. When building up a thickness, a layer of roving is alternated with a layer of mat, because the roving is so heavy that a bond between two layers of roving might leave voids. The mat fills in the dips and helps to level the roving surface for the next layer. Most repair projects involve relatively small areas, so the use of woven roving would be limited.

Specialty Fabrics

Specialized fiberglass products are available at some material-supply sources, but they are not essential for the do-it-yourselfer, particularly one who is learning to use the materials. Examples of these items include cloth that is described as unidirectional, biaxial, triaxial, and quadraxial, sometimes collectively called "knitted reinforcement" fabrics. In a unidirectional fabric, instead of being woven, the glass fibers are all parallel, held together by stitching. In biaxial fabric, two layers of unidirectional fibers are connected, with the fibers running at 45-degree angles to the fabric edge, and so on. The glass fibers may be stitched together, or a thin layer of another material is sewn to the top, holding the glass fibers in the desired direction or angle. "Biaxial fabric with mat" combines two fabric layers and one mat layer in one application. Tape can also be found in unidirectional and biaxial versions.

Similarly, alternatives to fiberglass reinforcement are often mentioned, particularly in descriptions of newer boats or newer technology, but these are not required for do-it-yourself projects. The two most often described are aramid (most people recognize the trade name Kevlar) and carbon fiber (also called graphite). These materials are chosen for their ability to increase stiffness and abrasion-resistance. The end product will also be much lighter in weight than a comparable item made with fiberglass fabric—an important factor in specialty construction but not necessary for ordinary fiberglass repairs.

✓ Glass is the component of a "fiberglass" composite that provides the strength.

✓ There are two kinds of fiberglass: E-glass is used in most boat construction and repair. S-glass is a more expensive product meant for structural applications. The local marine supply store will probably not have both kinds, so there should be no confusion; E-glass is the standard.

✓ Ordinary mat—the kind held together by the polyester-soluble binder—is sometimes called "roll mat." "Stitched mat," as the name suggests, is made without the use of a binder; the matted strands are held together by stitching them to an overlay of a very thin cloth.

✓ "Fabmat" or "biaxial with mat" describes the type of material made up of layers of fabric and mat that are already attached.

RESIN

Two basic types of resin are available. Both are referred to as "thermosetting" because they require the addition of a substance that causes the resin to heat and thereby cure.

Polyester and the newer vinylester are the same type of resin. Both are used with the same catalyst, methyl ethyl ketone peroxide (MEKP), which triggers the resin to cure. MEKP is a liquid, sold in small tubes along with the resin and also available separately. It is measured by drops or by cubic centimeters, the latter being the safer method when a sufficient quantity is being mixed to allow such measuring.

Epoxy is the second type of resin. It is combined with a hardener (also called amine curing agent) in a specific ratio (for example, 3:1 or 5:1). For repair purposes, the resin decision will most likely be between polyester and epoxy, but some description of vinylester will be given for general information.

"Catalyst" and "hardener" are different substances, but the terms are commonly used interchangeably.

Polyester Resin

Since most production boats are made with polyester resin, that might seem to be the most logical product to use for repair work, but opinions differ, with reason. Some people note that polyester has the poorest adhesion, is prone to shrinkage, is the least flexible, and may crack with stress. Despite these pessimistic observations, polyester is the most used and is considered generally suitable for most repairs. Once mixed with MEKP, polyester resin has a relatively short pot life (perhaps half an hour or less, depending somewhat on the temperature), so it should be mixed only in the quantity that can be used within the time frame. Polyester resins are subdivided into three types–laminating, finishing, and gelcoat.

Laminating Resin. Laminating or lay-up resin is used to build the thickness of fabric layers in a repair patch. This type of resin will not cure fully when exposed to air, but this is an advantage; it makes it possible to stop work on a project one day, then start again the next without sanding or making other preparation for a good bond between layers. The added coatings of resin will bond to the existing work.

When the laminated repair section has been built up to the desired thickness, the final coating of resin can be cured in one of two ways. One, the lay-up resin can be forced to cure by sealing out air. This can be done by spraying the tacky surface with polyvinyl alcohol (PVA), or by covering it tightly with a piece of plastic wrap. Once the surface is completely sealed and no air can get to it, the resin will cure. Two, a coat of finishing resin can be applied over the laminating resin.

Finishing Resin. The alternate way to complete the laminate is to use another type of polyester resin—the finishing resin. This product contains a substance that rises to the surface and so acts as the same kind of barrier as the PVA or the plastic wrap. It keeps air away from the resin; thus sealed from the air, the resin will cure.

Gelcoat. Gelcoat is the third type of polyester resin. As its name suggests, it is the finish coat; it is not meant to be used for the laminate. Precolored gelcoat can be purchased to match specific boat models, or separate pigments can be added to neutral gelcoat in a test of mix-and-try-to-match-it.

A thicker version of gelcoat is sold as "paste," useful as a combination filler and topcoat.

Vinylester Resin

Though used by manufacturers for some time, vinylester products are still not readily available to the amateur repair market. Vinylester is reputed to have better adhesion than standard polyester and also to be less prone to shrinkage. Perhaps most important, it is more moisture resistant; builders and repair yards often use vinylester on boat hulls to prevent blistering, a problem that affects many older fiberglass hulls (see chapter 8). Vinylester is capable of "stretching" as much as the glass fibers in the construction, so the finished composite will be less brittle than one made with polyester. Understandably, vinylester is more expensive than ordinary polyester resin. Some say it is more difficult to work with, being more affected by temperature and humidity. It is also difficult to sand when cured.

The mixing and application properties of vinylester are similar to those of polyester.

Epoxy Resin

Epoxy has long been acknowledged as the strongest, most water-resistant, and most flexible of the resins, therefore less prone to cracking under stress. (Today, manufacturers of vinylester resin make similar claims.) The shrinkage factor (that epoxy will NOT shrink noticeably) is a definite plus, particularly when a hull repair is below the waterline. Epoxy has better adhesive properties, another advantage for the secondary bonding of a below-waterline patch. Epoxy is expensive, and it requires a much longer cure time, so overall work time will be extended.

Different epoxy hardeners are available for use at different temperatures and/or to effect different cure times. Once mixed, epoxy remains workable for a considerably longer time than polyester, and as noted, the pot life can be somewhat controlled by the kind of hardener that is chosen.

Many factors must be weighed when deciding which material to use for which repair. One general overview holds that epoxy (and perhaps vinylester) is best where adhesive strength or moisture-resistance is most critical. Polyester is fine for general repairs, especially those above the waterline. A personal overview notes that the choice is often made according to which boatyard adviser is the most convincing on a given day.

✓ In the most general comparison, polyester resin (assuming finishing resin) can cure tack-free within an hour, but epoxy may require four or more.

✓ Polyester is much easier to sand when compared to either vinylester or epoxy.

✓ Polyester is less expensive than vinylester or epoxy.

✓ Epoxy is more waterproof than polyester. Vinylester is also very moisture resistant.

✓ Epoxy does not have as strong a solvent smell as polyester. Both are irritating to skin.

✓ Manufacturers can recommend approximate amounts of resin needed for laminating and for surface coats based on the type of fabric to be used and the area to be covered.

✓ With any fiberglassing materials, if there is any doubt about the suitability or compatibility of the product, call the manufacturer. Everyone wants a good result.

THICKENING AGENTS

Often, a repair requires the use of a putty-like substance to bond pieces together, to fill small holes and dents, or to level out a large surface in preparation for a finish coat. Such putties can be purchased in ready-to-mix tubes or cans, but it is just as easy to mix resin and a thickener in small amounts as needed. Besides the guaranteed material compatibility, this custom mixing allows the choice of different thickening agents to suit different purposes. Sometimes referred to as fillers, the following types of thickeners may be mixed—alone or in combination—with any kind of resin, to custom suit the project at hand.

Colloidal Silica

Colloidal silica is a fine, powdery substance that resembles baking soda. A small amount can be used to thicken resin only slightly in order to prevent the resin from sagging (called a "thixotropic" mix), or it can be mixed to a dense putty consistency for use when making structural repairs or modifications, such as bonding hardware or stringers. Colloidal silica is very lightweight—opening the can in a stiff wind is guaranteed to create a cloud of fluff. The putty mixture cures to a very hard substance that is not easy to sand.

Chopped Strand or Milled Glass Fibers

Bits of fiberglass fabric or mat chopped into tiny pieces will add strength to the putty and should be used in areas where this is critical (bonding stringers, filling gaps, etc.).

Microballoons

Microballoons or microspheres are tiny, lightweight, hollow plastic spheres. Putty made with these products is not meant for bonding—it will not be as strong as putty made with other thickeners—but when cured it is much easier to sand, and for this reason, it is especially popular for fairing large surfaces in preparation for the finish coat.

✓ Marine stores sell all varieties of filler putties, but polyester putty has long been the standard for auto body repair and is found at auto-parts stores in sizes ranging from tiny fix-it kits to gallon cans.

✓ In a pinch, talc (baby powder) or baking soda can be used to thicken resin. This option may be better than a trip to the boat store in the middle of a messy job. Generally, however, the finished job will benefit from the use of products made specifically for each application.

✓ To make "chopped strand," cut strips of mat about $\frac{1}{8}$ inch wide, then rub the strips together between fingertips until they fall apart.

✓ Mixed putty—even when thickened to peanut-butter consistency—should spread smoothly and not separate or pull apart as it is pushed along by the spreader. If it does separate, the putty contains too much thickener.

✓ No boat should be without a specialty putty called underwater epoxy. If it is necessary to make a repair quickly and the damaged area is wet and cannot be dried, underwater epoxy can be used to make an immediate repair; it will cure when wet. What starts as a temporary emergency repair often stays long enough to be regarded as the permanent fix.

PIGMENT

Color can be added to laminating or finishing resins as well as to gelcoat. Small bottles of pigment are sold in a range of colors, including a choice of whites. Though tinting the resin or gelcoat is a good idea in theory, it does not always bring perfection, for the obvious reason that even the company-matched color, which is fresh and new, will appear to be different from the color on the boat, which is faded or chalked. Still, it is a better starting point than navy gray. And often, a few coats of wax over the entire surface will help to visually blend the new color.

Pigments may be labeled for product compatibility, but most can be used with either polyester or epoxy resin. The choice of color additives specifically marked for use with epoxy seems limited, but Gougeon Brothers tested other products and reports success with many possibilities, including powdered tempera paint and Rit liquid dye. MAS Epoxies recommends artists' acrylic paints.

SOLVENTS AND CLEANERS

It should not be necessary to thin resin, so solvent use for this purpose is strongly discouraged by manufacturers. But even though thinning is unnecessary, a solvent wash is often recommended before applying resin to a newly sanded repair surface and sometimes between coats, when using epoxy resin.

When working with polyester resin, surfaces can be cleaned by wiping them with isopropyl (denatured) alcohol, lacquer thinner, or styrene. Acetone use is common, even though it is discouraged by many because of possible impurities.

When working with epoxy, acetone was the favored cleaning agent for years, but today, it is recommended that an acetone wipe should be immediately followed by a clean-rag wipe, before the solvent has a chance to air dry. (The reason for this caution is that commercially available acetone is not pure, so it is important to remove any residue that might interfere with a good bond between coats of resin.) Alcohol or plain water can be used to clean surfaces.

Other cleaning supplies include a degreaser and a dewaxer (to remove oily dirt and wax from fiberglass surfaces before starting a repair), waterless soap (for hands and clothing), white vinegar (to clean uncured epoxy resin from hands, clothing, and tools), plain water, and liquid detergent.

✓ Some epoxy manufacturers sell a special solvent to use as a surface decontaminant as well as a tool cleaner.

✓ Though acetone is sold as an epoxy thinner, using it for that purpose could affect the strength and moisture resistance of the epoxy.

✓ Toluene can be used as a dewaxer; methyl ethyl ketone (MEK) is a degreaser.

Chapter 2

Tools

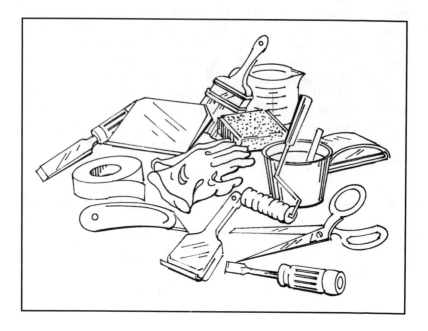

Most of the tools needed for fiberglass repairs are already on the shelf in the workshop of a typical do-it-yourselfer. Not all the items listed in this chapter will be used on every job, but it is helpful to see what might be needed at different stages of the process.

CUTTING FABRIC

Fiberglass cloth is available in so many types and weights, even cutting the fabric may require a certain amount of practice. Each person soon finds which tool works best for which job.

Scissors

It may be tempting to use an old pair of scissors, but that would be a serious mistake. Dull scissors cannot make a clean cut, and if scissors are rusted or the blades nicked, the fiberglass cloth will catch on those rough spots and quickly become a mess of pulls and crimps and ravels, making it more difficult to leave a smooth, neat surface when saturating it with resin. Starting with a pair of clean, sharp, possibly new, probably dedicated scissors is essential.

Utility Knife

Some people call this tool a mat knife. Whatever its name, the traditional fat-handled type uses easily replaceable single-edged blades that are conveniently stored in the take-apart handle of the knife. Another type of utility knife has a breakaway blade, again making it simple to ensure a new cutting edge. The blade can be renewed as often as necessary, and it is desirable to do so often. The knife can be used instead of scissors to cut fabric, particularly when larger straight sides are desired. A metal yardstick or T-square held tightly over the fabric can be used as a cutting guide. The knife will also be used to trim the edges of fiberglass cloth after the resin has partially cured, either to make a neat seam where fabric pieces butt together or to remove excess fabric from the edges of the repair. If the blade is not sharp and clean, it too will catch and crimp the fabric, just at the curing stage when it should not be disturbed.

MEASURING AND MIXING RESIN

According to resin manufacturers, errors in measuring and/or incomplete mixing are the source of the great majority of problems encountered by new fiberglass workers.

Measuring Polyester

When using polyester products, resin is measured by the ounce and MEKP (the mixing agent that causes polyester resin to cure) is measured either by cubic centimeters (marked on the tube container) or by drops (counted carefully as they drip from the MEKP tube or an eye dropper; the required amount is only 1 to 2% of the amount of resin). For the resin, a transparent kitchen measuring cup has quantities clearly marked and visible from any side, and marine stores sell suitably marked plastic cups.

Measuring Epoxy

Epoxy resin and its hardener are mixed to a given ratio, for example, 3:1 or 5:1. Measuring has been simplified by the manufacturers who provide special pumps that replace the caps on the resin and hardener cans.

Mixing

Pots. Small cardboard buckets may be purchased for mixing resins. For epoxy, plastic water bottles can be used with the top half cut off so the resin in the wide "pot" portion can be mixed easily. Similarly, two-liter soda bottles can be cut down to use the bottom portion. When working with polyester, however, plastic bottles may be a poor choice, as the resin may soften or melt some plastic material. A few test globs of resin should indicate which plastics to avoid.

✓ Metal and glass containers can get very hot because of the heat generated by the resin after it is mixed.

✓ Don't use a Styrofoam cup to measure polyester—the resin will melt the cup.

✓ Don't use paper cups that are waxed. The wax will melt into the resin and may affect the curing properties.

Stir sticks. Traditionally, wooden "ice cream" sticks were the standard mixers. Or maybe a pencil or a plain old wooden stick. However, the paint on pencils often melts with resin, and sticks tend to leave slivers. Now, plastic stir sticks are the new standard. They're easily cleaned for reuse, and since one end of the stick is straight instead of curved, it may do a better job of coaxing all of the resin out of the measuring cup.

Plastic lids. Small amounts of putty can be mixed on any kind of flat plastic or wood surface, but the lids from cottage cheese or deli salad containers are easy to use and easy to throw away. Cut them in half so the putty knife can be scraped against a straight edge.

APPLYING RESIN

Resin can be applied with brush or roller, or it can be poured onto the surface and moved over the fabric quickly with a plastic spreader.

Brush

Throwaway bristle brushes are the most practical type of brush to use for all kinds of resin. Considering the number of brushes that may be used on a single repair, it may seem wasteful to toss them, but it takes a lot of solvent to clean one brush thoroughly, and then there is the added problem of what to do with the dirty solvent. Factor in time, and it is understandable why the manufacturers of throwaways are only too happy to provide an ample supply.

✓ Foam brushes cannot be used with polyester—they will melt. Even with epoxy, some brands may soften.

Roller

Roller application of resin is more applicable to larger projects, like building a boat or putting a protective layer of fiberglass over a wooden surface. Most repair work is not that big a job, but there are times when a small roller might be useful. As with brushes, foam rollers can be used with epoxy, but not with polyester.

The roller material must be compatible with fiberglass products—many are labeled for such use. Using an ordinary paint roller may add unwanted texture to the repair, as the roller nap separates from the core. The handle of a roller can be reused and should be cleaned before the resin cures, but the roller itself is another throwaway.

Grooved Metal Roller

Whether resin is initially brushed or rolled, the grooved roller is the necessary follow-up tool. After the cloth has been saturated, this roller is used to level the amount of resin on the cloth to ensure a good bond. It pushes away resin from areas that are overloaded, thereby preventing the cloth from floating off the surface on a puddle of resin.

Spreader

Some people call this a "squeegee," but its function is to spread putty or resin. This flat piece of plastic has a beveled edge that can push repair putty into all the dings on a marred surface or else level out the liquid resin just poured onto a piece of cloth. Usually packaged in three sizes, spreaders are always available at the auto-parts store if the marine supply is sold out. It is advisable to keep many spares; once a spreader gets a rough edge, it is useless on cloth. In theory, it is possible to sand the edge of a spreader, but since the plastic tends to warp after some use, attempting to put a new edge on an old spreader might put that activity in the same category as cleaning brushes—not really worth the time.

Syringes

Syringes are used with epoxy resin mixtures to inject the material into otherwise inaccessible places. When filling deep screw holes, the syringe guarantees the resin mix will reach to the bottom. When repairing cored decks, the syringe helps to get the epoxy mix to the bottom of the repair as well as into any gaps between the core and the skins.

SANDING

Sanding is necessary at both ends of a repair project. First, sanding clears a damaged area for a proper repair. Once the patching is complete, sanding prepares the surface for a proper finish. And the finest sanding of all takes place AFTER the final coat has been applied.

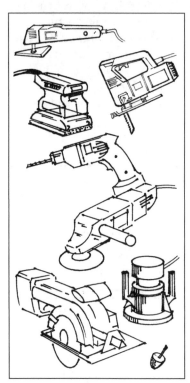

Power Tools

The type of damage to be fixed will determine the kind of tools that are required to prepare the area for repair. A circular saw or saber saw might be needed to cut away a section of crushed fiberglass that is beyond repair. Or perhaps a grinder can remove a damaged section in stages, working down to the place where the laminate is still intact. For a relatively small hole or void, a Dremel-type rotary tool with a grinding burr can quickly clean up a ragged surface or edge. The same kind of bitt on an electric drill might be sufficient for certain repairs. A vibrating sander is useful for finishing work, and the triangular "mouse" sander is great for angling into hard-to-reach places. Buffing can be done with the appropriate pad on an orbital buffer/polisher.

Sanding Aids

Small repair projects require only the use of a small hand-sanding block. Perhaps the most commonly used is the hard-rubber type that has prongs to hold the sandpaper in place. Even more basic is a small rectangle of wood wrapped with sandpaper held in place by a gloved hand.

If any large areas need to be sanded, fairing is accomplished with the help of a larger block or sanding board, a slightly flexible piece of wood about 17 inches long and 4 inches wide with sandpaper glued to the bottom. Two "handles" (small blocks of wood shaped enough to be easy to grasp) should be attached to the top near each end, enabling the sander to hold and sand with long strokes.

Spreaders can be put to use at the sanding stage of a repair too. Sandpaper wrapped around the edge of a spreader can remove a high spot quickly while being held in an almost flat position to avoid hill-and-dale sanding. A similarly wrapped handled spreader (wide plastic putty knife) can reach into hard-to-access corners and grooves.

Sandpaper

It's a surprise for first-time workers to see how much of a sandpaper inventory may be required for an apparently simple job. First, sanding disks or other shapes must be purchased to match each of the power tools. Next, flat sheets must be handy to cut apart for use with sanding blocks or the long sanding board. For the initial repair phase, all of the papers should be available in grits from about 60 to 220. Occasionally, an even coarser grit might be required. For the final work on finish coats, whether gelcoat or paint, a supply of wet-or-dry paper up to 600 or even 1200 may be necessary, depending on the perfectionist level of the worker.

✓ It's not possible to recommend a general type of paper since many brands, good and poor, use the same type of abrasive. Personal favorites, by the easiest identification of color, are 3M products: green for the heavy-duty sanding of clearing damaged areas and gold for the patched repair. (Company literature describes purple "Imperial" paper as even better than green for heavy surface removal; it cuts fast and is less likely to load up.) Wet/dry papers are not differentiated by color.

✓ Before buying a large quantity of an unknown brand of sandpaper, buy single sheets and test their effectiveness: How well do they do the job? Do they load up with sanding dust too quickly? How long do they last?

Given the need for so many kinds of paper, the temptation is to head for the discount hardware or home store and stock up. But that would be a mistake. Good sandpaper should be used for all purposes, "good" meaning a brand name and the type specifically recommended for the job at hand. Cheap papers not only waste money, but precious time and effort as well.

FINAL FINISHING

Gelcoat

For the typically small area of a repair, if the finish coat is to be gelcoat, it can be applied with a putty knife or spreader. Depending on the type of gelcoat used, it may need to be sealed from the air with a piece of plastic wrap. (Gelcoat can be sprayed, but this is usually done only by professionals.)

Paint

If the finish coat is to be paint, it CAN be sprayed. Small spray bottles with aerosol attachments make such touch-ups not only possible but almost easy. The Preval Paint Sprayer can be found in many kinds of stores: marine, hardware, auto-parts, even some home supply warehouses.

If paint is to be brushed, then a good quality bristle brush is essential (badger is still a favorite). The most recommended paint to top a fiberglass repair is a two-part polyurethane. Whether overcoating polyester or epoxy, the proper primer must be used to ensure the best bond.

Compounding or Polishing

Very fine wet-or-dry sandpaper is used on finish coats of gelcoat and some paints to remove drips, runs, orange-peels, and other blemishes in the coating. These papers will leave the surface smooth but slightly dull, showing more of a satin finish than the desired high gloss. The next step in finishing is the application of rubbing compound or polishing compound. These are wax-like products that contain a very fine abrasive (generally "rubbing" compound will have a coarser abrasive than "polishing"). Applied like wax, the compounds are then buffed out to a flawless surface, resulting in a gleaming mirror shine. At least that is the ideal. Once again, the extent of buffing will depend on the image in the mind of the buffer. A buffing pad on an electric drill or sander must be used with caution; if rpms are too high, the compound may get hot, and that could ruin the desired effect. Some people insist that hand buffing is the only way to achieve perfection, but low rpm buffers are used with success.

✓ For retouch sanding of gelcoat or paint defects, a perfect tool is a small flexible block found at the automotive paint store. It levels high spots and paint mistakes without "dipping" the surrounding area, leaving a perfect surface.

✓ Whether the repair is topped with paint or gelcoat, the final finish for hull or cabin side (not deck) is usually a coat or two of a quality wax. Check with the paint manufacturer on the use of wax, as some think it's unnecessary.

Miscellaneous Supplies

The following items may also be useful:

- Screwdriver
- Chisel
- Files (round and flat)
- Pointed-end can opener
- Masking tape
- Plastic film (food wrap; used when curing gelcoat)
- Heat gun or hair dryer
- Router
- Abrasive pads
- Plain white rags
- Safety supplies (see chapter 3)

Chapter 3

Cautions

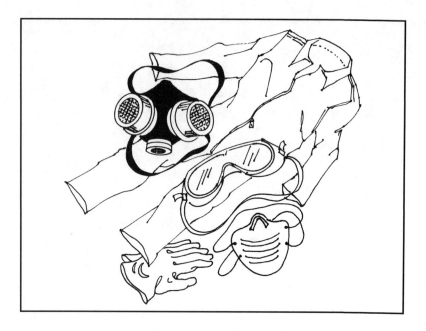

It's easy to ignore safety suggestions, rationalizing that only full-time fiberglass workers need to be concerned about overexposure. However, anyone who has been unfortunate enough to develop a fiberglass rash will no longer ignore preventive measures. The rash may be similar to the one caused by poison ivy, but it stings as much as it itches. Some individuals are particularly sensitive and, after an initial bout with the condition, are forever afflicted even with the smallest amount of exposure. The cautions are justified; there's nothing to be gained by tempting fate in the form of fiberglass and resin.

Besides the possibility of skin irritation, an overdose of resin fumes can cause unpleasant side effects, perhaps more subtle initially, but still problematic—headache, burning eyes, irritation to nose and throat, even nausea. As with exposure to many chemicals, long-term exposure can have a cumulative affect.

CLOTHING COVER-UPS

As already noted, the simple act of cutting fiberglass fabric releases tiny glass slivers into the air. Sanding, both before and after the actual fiberglass work, naturally produces more grit and sends out more particles. To stem this flying debris cloud, power tools should be attached to a vacuum cleaner (some have their own built-in vac), but when cutting fabric or hand-sanding, the fiberglass worker must heed all the warnings and make every effort to prevent the fiberglass bits and sandpaper grit from settling on the skin, including the scalp.

Coveralls are certainly right for the job, and today it's possible to buy a whole supply of disposables in this category too. More often, the sometime boat worker has a number of outfits that have stepped down the wardrobe chain to become boatyard clothes. Long-sleeved shirts and long pants will catch the sanding dust, fiberglass chips, and resin drips. For some projects, an entire set of clothing might be set aside for throwaway.

Disposable gloves should be purchased by the box of one hundred. They disappear very quickly, prompting frequent checks for a dwindling supply. The fiberglass rash is not the only risk when working without gloves; the skin can also absorb the chemicals in the resin products. If tool cleaning involves working with solvents, use solvent-proof gloves, not the thin latex disposables.

✓ Before starting any fiberglass project, coat hands with a barrier cream. If resin does get on the skin, through a hole in a glove, for example, hands will be easier to clean and skin will suffer less.

✓ Don't use solvent to clean epoxy from hands. Use a waterless hand cleaner instead, followed by lots of soap and water.

✓ White vinegar will remove uncured epoxy from tools and clothes—and skin, if necessary. So will isopropyl alcohol. But once the resin is gone, wash the cleaners off with soap and water.

✓ If the work area is not close to a water source, keep at least a one-gallon bottle of water nearby, along with some hand soap or dish detergent. These may be needed for some emergency washing and rinsing.

Fabric or leather-reinforced work gloves should be worn when sanding or scraping. Gardening gloves are a good compromise. They are tough enough to resist abrasive sandpapers, but fitted enough to allow easier working.

A hat or bandanna—or both—completes the fiberglassing ensemble and should be included, even if it's August in Florida.

FACIAL PROTECTION

With the right kind of clothing, skin will be protected, but the face needs special attention.

Eyes should be shielded with either safety goggles or eyeglasses. Many workers keep an old pair of prescription glasses for just such a reason. While the prescription may be slightly out-of-date, the lenses are usually good enough for work purposes and they provide good protection for the eyes. Naturally, this also keeps the new eyeglasses free from resin-melt.

Anyone who is particularly sensitive to noise should consider using earplugs when working with power tools for a long period of time.

It would be impossible to avoid breathing some of the sanding dust, so some type of face mask must be worn. A dust mask will keep the larger grit particles out of the nose, but when working with resin, better protection will be found with a respirator-type mask, which can halt resin fumes as well as sanding particles.

Respirator masks can be fitted with different types of cartridges, but no matter what type is to be used, in order for the mask to do its job, it must fit properly. Many men have found that a beard interferes with that fit.

✓ If resin splashes into the eyes, flush them gently but thoroughly with water. If they continue to feel irritated, get to a doctor quickly.

✓ If all the dust masks that were stowed in the locker have mysteriously disappeared, at least tie a bandanna or other cloth snugly over nose and mouth. While not a particularly good mask, it is better than nothing at all.

✓ To minimize airborne grit, use power tools that can be attached to vacuum cleaner hoses. The actual methods of attachment are sometimes iffy, but duct tape often helps.

✓ Sometimes it is impractical to attach the vacuum cleaner directly to the sander or grinder (for example, if the vacuum has a short hose, the normal movement of the sander will pull the vacuum over on its side, stopping the suction). Tape the vacuum hose to the deck or other work area, and move the hose occasionally as the sanding progresses.

VENTILATION

If the repair project means working inside the boat, good ventilation must be established before starting. All ports and hatches should be opened and onboard exhausting fans turned on. The resin should be mixed outside the boat, to keep the odor out as long as possible, particularly when working with polyester resin. A large window "box" fan can be positioned in such a way that it pushes out polyester fumes as it pulls in outside air. Eye protection is even more important when working inside the boat; in close quarters, it's practically guaranteed that resin will drip or splash.

MORE CAUTIONS

If a person is already sensitive to paint products, it would probably be foolish to take on a fiberglass repair project. Stores that sell the materials for fiberglass work should be able to provide Material Safety Data Sheets (MSDS), which contain safety-related information on resins and their solvents.

The data sheets note any regulated or hazardous ingredients, and include information on working with the product: incompatibility with other products, health hazard data, flammability, spill procedures, general precautions. (If for some reason the store cannot provide the data sheets, check the websites or call the toll-free information directory for phone numbers of resin manufacturers.)

✓ On a really hot day, the resin-mixing pot must be watched very closely after the hardener has been added. Because of the concentration of resin in a confined area, heat develops quickly in the container, and in rare instances, the mix may start to smoke as it begins the thermosetting process in a probably accelerated time frame. Don't try to hurry the work project in order to use the rapidly curing resin—it's already too late. Immediately remove the container from the boat and set it in an out-of-the-way spot until the resin cures completely. Save the resin rock for a paperweight or bookend.

✓ Resins and solvents are flammable. Smoking around these products is dangerous. The work area must be kept clear of any possible source of spark.

Chapter 4

Methods

When working with fiberglass, the same repair techniques are applied to many different types of damage. While some repetition is unavoidable, the general instructions for handling the materials are briefly given here; later chapters will provide step-by-step guidance for specific projects and will include special or unique directions as needed. Not every repair will require every technique—for an obvious example, simple nicks don't require the use of fabric—but many will be common to many repairs.

Basic steps:

- Prepare the damaged area for repair
- Fill dents and gaps, add supports
- Cut fabric
- Measure and mix resin
- Apply resin to fabric
    Brush, roll, or pour
    Laminate layers
- Sand
- Apply finish coat
    Gelcoat
    Primer and paint
- Cleanup

PREPARE THE DAMAGED AREA

All projects begin with cleaning the area to be repaired, and cleaning can encompass anything from simple washing to sawing a new edge for a patch. In addition to washing the surface area, a dewaxer should be used to remove all traces of waxy compounds that could interfere with the bonding of the repair materials.

Even for relatively minor gelcoat repairs, the existing surface must be scuffed enough to dull the shine, so the new material will adhere properly. If fiberglass fabric is to be applied, it will be necessary to remove the gelcoat entirely in order to bond new fiberglass to the original laminate. (A disk sander or a sanding pad on a drill will do the job, using coarse, 40- to 60-grit paper.) A grinding burr can be used to create a clean, beveled edge around a hole. A saw could remove a chunk of badly damaged composite, or a router could cut away the top skin of a sandwich construction in order to remove a bad core. Each project will dictate the required task and the appropriate tools.

When patching a hole, particularly one that is completely through the hull, all sections of damaged fiberglass composite must be cut away. The hole should be enlarged as much as is necessary to reach solid laminate, leaving a round or oblong shape to fill with new fiberglass. The entire perimeter of the hole should be beveled to create a wider surface for the bond between the new material and the existing laminate. A 12:1 ratio (sloped edge to thickness of laminate) is recommended: if the hull thickness is ¼-inch thick, the bevel should span 3 inches. If the hull is ½", the bevel would be 6 inches, and so on.

The grit from sanding, grinding, or sawing must be completely removed by vacuuming, washing, and wiping dry. If polyester resin will be used, the surface can be wiped with acetone, lacquer thinner, isopropyl (denatured) alcohol, or styrene. If epoxy resin will be used, the rag should be dampened with alcohol or water. Although for years acetone was the cleaner-of-choice for epoxy too,

Prepare the damaged area; if necessary, grind off all gelcoat.

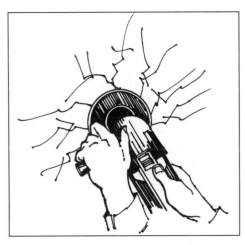

today it is mentioned only with the following caveat: wipe the acetone away immediately with a clean cloth before it has a chance to evaporate to ensure that no solvent residue is left on the surface that might interfere with the bonding of the resin.

FILL THE NICKS AND GAPS

To smooth a surface for cosmetic reasons or in preparation for adding fiberglass cloth, all dents and scrapes must be filled in and leveled off. This patching can be done with thickened resin that is "mixed-to-order" or with a commercially packaged putty (filler), available in formulations of polyester, vinylester, or epoxy. A plastic spreader held at about a 45-degree angle works well to fill the dents without leaving a lot of excess putty; naturally a putty knife could also be used (handled plastic putty knives are a handy compromise and are available in many sizes). In rare instances, one application of filler will be sufficient; however, in most cases, two or three applications will be required. When filling a deep dent, each application of putty should add no more than $\frac{1}{8}$" thickness, and each layer should dry thoroughly before the next is applied. A final sanding should leave a perfectly smooth and level surface. Microballoons make the best filler for this overall fairing.

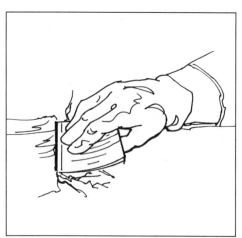

Fill the nicks and dents with putty made from resin and a thickening agent.

✓ Fiberglassing instructions often call for putty to be mixed to a certain consistency for a particular job, using such obvious comparisons as "ketchup," "mayonnaise," or "peanut butter."

✓ Regardless of which thickener is chosen, always mix the resin and its curing agent thoroughly before adding the thickener.

✓ When fiberglass will be used to cover a stringer or to reinforce the seam where a bulkhead meets the hull side or cabin sole, use thick putty (peanut-butter consistency) to round the joint where the two parts meet. This rounded seam of filler putty is called a fillet, and it must be made before applying cloth because the fabric cannot bend over or into a sharp 90-degree corner. After slathering putty into the seam, use an ice-cream stick (for its rounded end) or the back of a teaspoon, and drag it along the seam in a slow but steady motion to create a neat, uniform U-shape to the seam. Scrape away excess putty from the top and bottom of the seam to keep future sanding to a minimum.

✓ After spreading putty to fill dents, clean up the excess from around the patch while it is still workable. This will shorten future sanding time considerably. Epoxy especially is a lot easier to scrape off when it's still uncured than to sand off when set.

CUT THE FABRIC

It is desirable to cut all the fabric pieces needed for a repair before starting the resin application. Ideally, enough fabric pieces should be cut to create the same thickness as the section being patched. Since it is doubtful the first guess on the number of pieces will be accurate, it's best to overestimate, mainly because it is such a disruption to stop in the middle of the sticky laminating process in order to cut more neat, clean pieces of fiberglass cloth.

If the repair involves filling a round hole, the fabric pieces will not all be cut the same diameter, because the edges of the hole have been sanded to the bevel. Thus the size of each fabric piece will vary a bit from the one before, to fill the changing diameter of the hole. If the patch is a slightly irregular shape, a pattern can be made and traced onto the cloth, but the fabric pieces will still vary in size as the repair thickness builds.

Fiberglass cloth can be marked lightly with a felt-tip pen to help guide the cutting process. The ink will probably dissolve with the resin, producing an unexpected colored streak or two, but this should not be a problem in lay-up stages. The ink will cure into the resin and eventually be covered by the final finish coats.

For most repair projects, the size of the cloth pieces will be small enough that scissors will be the most practical tool for cutting.

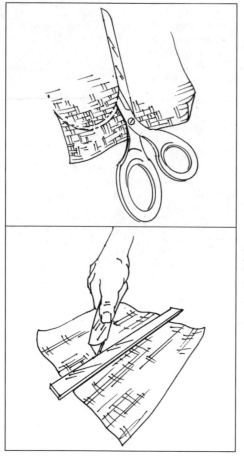

Use new, good quality
scissors to cut fabric.

Cut fabric with a utility
knife; use a metal
straightedge for a guide.

However, for applications covering a large surface, a mat knife
may be handy, used with a metal straightedge.

All the fiberglass pieces—woven fabric, mat, or combination—
should be cut and placed in a convenient (reachable) location, laid
out in the order in which they will be used.

✓ To establish a straight line for cutting standard cross weave fiberglass cloth, remove
  one strand from the width of the cloth. Cut a slit at one side to get a good grip on the
  strand; hold the fabric down with one hand while the other pulls the strand.

✓ It has been suggested that "standard" mat should not be used if the repair will be done with epoxy resin because the mat strands are held together by a binder that dissolves with polyester resin but not epoxy. Stitched mat could provide an alternative—no binder, no problem. However, according to tests by Gougeon Brothers no difference was found in the curing of an epoxy repair done with standard "styrene-soluble-binder" mat or one that used stitched mat. Apparently, the binder simply cures in and does not affect the strength of the repair.

✓ When using mat, the fabric can often be torn apart rather than cut with scissors. Frayed edges of the mat allow easier blending or bonding between layers.

✓ For strength on a larger patch, the orientation of fabric layers can be staggered. For example, after the first layer is in place, rotate the fabric on the second layer so the weave is at a 45-degree angle to the first layer, similar to the way biaxial cloth is made.

✓ When choosing what kind of fabric to use, consider that the heavier the fabric weight, the harder it will be to saturate with resin. The strength of the composite will be comparable whether it is built up with many thin layers or a few heavy layers.

✓ When estimating the number of fabric pieces required to build a specific thickness, it is possible to make an educated guess. Manufacturers can provide thickness figures for different weights of fabric. Divide the desired overall thickness by the single-layer thickness and cut that many pieces. (Plus a few!)

MEASURE AND MIX THE RESIN

The resin cans, catalyst or hardener, measuring cups, mixing pots, mixing sticks, thickeners, and pigment should all be assembled in one spot. An appropriately sized corrugated cardboard box will keep all resin supplies conveniently together. The front of the box can be cut down about half way for easier access. When the workday is done, cleanup is fairly easy. Cans are closed up, a piece of cardboard is propped into the cutout side, and the box is covered and moved to a protected spot where it will be shaded from the next day's morning sun. If work will be resumed soon, the resin-measuring cups can be saved in small plastic bags (because the remaining contents will still be sticky) and left in the box too. The box goes wherever the next project leads. A box of disposable gloves should be part of the work kit.

Polyester resin is measured by the ounce, and its catalyst, methyl ethyl ketone peroxide (MEKP), is measured by cubic centimeters or drops according to manufacturer's directions. Once measured, the resin is poured (and scraped) into the mixing pot. The measuring cup should be used for resin only; the resin-scraping

Polyester resin is mixed with methyl ethyl ketone peroxide, or MEKP. Epoxy resin is mixed with a hardener. Different types of hardeners are available for use in different applications.

stick can be placed into the cup to be ready for the next use. Labeling the stick is not as silly as it may sound. If a stick is used to mix resin and catalyst, it must be kept out of the resin-measuring container, to prevent even a trace amount of catalyst from getting into the resin cup.

Epoxy resin is mixed according to a given ratio of resin to hardener, but instead of pouring out specified amounts into separate measuring cups, manufacturers provide pumps to replace the caps on the cans, making the measuring aspect nearly foolproof. One stroke on the hardener pump brings the right amount of hardener to mix with resin provided by one stroke on the resin pump.

If no pumps are available, measuring can be done with two paper cups, one for resin and one for hardener. If the cups are not marked to show amounts, a tape line can be used to indicate the correct number of ounces (for example, three ounces for the resin cup and one ounce for the hardener cup). To determine where the tape lines should be placed, a measuring cup and water can be used to measure the correct amounts, first for the resin cup, then for the hardener cup. After the water is poured into the respective cup, the outside is marked with the tape, the water is tossed, and the cup is dried thoroughly. This measuring method is messier than working with the pumps, but it works.

As soon as the two components are in the container, mixing should begin. Stir at least one full minute and preferably two. The sides of the container and the stir stick should be scraped often.

✓ When measuring resin and its hardener or catalyst, it is important to strive for accurate amounts. Though there may be a small margin for error, a mix that is too far off may never cure. This seemingly simple step prompts many calls to the technical hotline for help. Unfortunately, it can make the difference between doing a great job or having to scrape away goo and start all over again.

✓ Less catalyst is better than too much. If too much is added, the resin will kick (start to cure) too quickly, which can result in a weak bond or an exceptionally brittle laminate.

✓ After mixing, resin that is still in the container will start to cure before resin that is spread out onto fabric because in the confines of the container, more heat is generated. This is an "exothermic reaction"; the material is "thermosetting" because of its heat-curing capacity.

✓ When adding thickeners or pigments to resin, first mix the resin with catalyst or hardener, then add the thickener and/or pigment.

✓ For comparison purposes in the broadest, approximate terms: Working time for polyester resin after mixing—20 to 45 minutes; for epoxy—1 to 2 hours.

✓ When using measuring pumps for epoxy, one caution should be observed. If, after initial use, a pump sits idle for a while, the first pump stroke may not provide the correct measure; the pump may need to be primed with one test stroke before trusting its measure. To test, pump into a clean can so the resin or hardener can be returned to the original container after the test measure.

✓ When using epoxy resin, choose the hardener that best suits the job. Fast cure, slow cure, or clear cure (the latter necessary only when applying cloth over a wood surface when the intention is to allow the wood grain to show).

✓ Mark the measuring cups and their respective scraping sticks (as well as can lids, when applicable) with color-matched tape or ink spots to keep like products and tools together.

✓ Epoxy can be measured another way if the mixing pot has vertical (not slanted) sides. Use a straight-bottomed stick (like a paint stirring stick). If the resin/hardener ratio is a 5:1 mix, mark off six same-size increments, starting at the bottom of the stick. Hold the stick upright in the container, bottom of stick touching bottom of container. Pour resin up to the top of mark number five, then add hardener until the contents of the can touches mark number six. Mix thoroughly, scraping the stir stick as well as the sides of the mixing pot often. Reuse the stir stick but scrape and clean it between mixings.

✓ So-called ideal temperature for using epoxy is about 70 degrees. For every ten degrees the temperature rises, the working time may be cut by as much as half.

APPLY RESIN TO CLOTH

Cloth is bonded to a repair surface by the wet method ("paint" a coat of resin onto the surface before positioning the cloth) or the dry method (place the cloth in position, then saturate it from the top). It can also be saturated before moving it into position, but this

A roller provides a fast
way to apply resin to cloth.

can get very messy on large jobs. Which way to work is mainly a matter of personal preference; some practice with each method will establish a favorite, and the type of job may also suggest the best method for a particular repair.

Depending on the size of the job, resin is applied by brush, roller, or the flat plastic spreaders that some people call squeegees. The latter are usually reserved for large jobs.

A stiff bristle brush works well to "push" thick resin into the cloth. Throwaway bristle brushes are ideal; the bristles can be cut shorter if they seem too flexible.

Rollers are practical to force resin into cloth (the 3-inch rollers are handy for small jobs). Large rollers and spreaders can move a lot of resin quickly, after it has been poured onto an expanse of cloth. Short nap rollers should be used with polyester resin, and urethane foam rollers with epoxy.

Resin should be applied to fiberglass cloth in a sufficient amount to saturate the fabric completely. The cloth becomes transparent when it is saturated, so there can be no doubt about whether enough resin has been applied.

The first coat of resin will not fill all of the cloth weave, and no attempt should be made to do so at this stage. Too much resin on the initial coating could cause an unexpected problem: if excess resin accumulates in puddles underneath the cloth, the fiberglass may actually float off the surface rather than bond to it. The puddled areas will show as more shiny (wetter-looking); the properly saturated fabric will have a matte finish. Later, after the final layer of fiberglass has been applied, three or four coats of resin can be added. These will fill the fabric weave and then add a thick, protective coating of resin over the cloth, so future sanding cannot break through to the fabric.

To build up a thick fiberglass patch, many layers of material will be used. Woven fabric can be used exclusively for this layering, though this could be the more time-consuming choice, depending on the weight of the cloth. Mat will create a thickness faster than cloth alone, but the layering should be done by alternating pieces of cloth and mat. Other options for a quick buildup include woven roving or a fabric that combines layers of cloth and mat in one piece of material.

When using polyester resin, this "lay-up" will be done with the laminating-type resin. Three or four layers of fabric can be applied, saturating each individually. These layers should be allowed to cure partially before adding more. The laminating resin will not cure completely while it is exposed to air (it will harden, but the surface will be tacky), so multiple layers of fiberglass and resin can be applied without cleaning or sanding between layers. The final coat can be done with a finishing resin, which DOES cure, or a final coat of laminating resin can be "forced" to cure by sealing out the air. This is done either by spraying the surface with polyvinyl alcohol (PVA) or by taping a piece of plastic wrap over the surface.

When using epoxy resin, apply three or four layers of fabric, saturating each and removing excess resin; then allow the resin to cure partially. While it is still tacky, add more pieces of fabric, and repeat the process until the desired thickness has been reached. In order to build a protective coating of resin over the fiberglass cloth, subsequent coats of resin can be painted without cleaning or sanding as long as they are added while the last coat is still a bit tacky. Once the last coat has cured tack-free, the surface of the cured resin must be cleaned of the waxy coating ("amine blush") that rises to the top as epoxy cures. A rag dampened with water will do the job. After this cleaning, the surface should be sanded lightly in preparation for the finish work. At this time, any dents or dips in the surface should be filled with a putty of thickened resin; alternate filling and sanding will ultimately create the smooth, even surface that is required for applying the final finish.

✓ To make epoxy flow easier, especially in cool weather, warm it. Use a heat lamp or keep the epoxy in a warm place until ready to use.

✓ In a repair situation, epoxy and vinylester can be used over polyester, but polyester should not be used over epoxy. (An exception would be gelcoat. With proper preparation, it is possible to apply gelcoat over epoxy, though most new fiberglass workers choose not to try.)

✓ Though thinning of resin is generally not recommended (it would compromise the strength of the finished laminate), some people add a small amount of thinner to a final coat of resin, for a smoother result.

✓ When polyester resin is used with ordinary fiberglass mat, the material becomes softer as the binder dissolves, allowing it to drape around curves more readily. When this same mat is wet out with epoxy resin, it will retain its stiffness, but for some jobs (when working on a deck or cabin top—any area with minimum curve), the stiffness can be an advantage.

✓ For small repairs, it is unlikely that fabric pieces would need to be overlapped, but if someday it is necessary to cover an area that is wider than the fabric roll, there is a way to avoid the bump that would result from a double thickness of fabric. As the fabric is applied to the surface, overlap the two pieces about an inch. When the resin is partially cured (slightly tacky and soft enough so a fingernail can still make a dent), use a mat knife to cut a straight line through both pieces of fabric. The blade must cut cleanly through both layers or the desired seamless result will be ragged instead. Remove the cutaway portion of the top fabric. Then lift the edge of the top fabric just enough to get to the bottom cloth, and take out the cutaway portion of that cloth. Smooth the top layer back in place, adding a small amount of resin if necessary and rolling it down to ensure a good bond. As might be expected, this step may take a bit of practice—or at the very least, some prior observation of one of the fiberglass artists at work.

✓ When using a brush to apply resin to cloth, it will usually be used in a dabbing motion rather than a brushing motion.

✓ If using fiberglass tape to strengthen a seam, center the tape over the seam and add sufficient coats of resin to fill and cover the weave. Fair the edges into the surface using resin thickened with microballoons.

✓ Neither fabric nor tape will fold around a 90-degree corner—no matter how many times it is pushed down, it will eventually lift, leaving a giant bubble to be repaired later. Fold the tape around the corner, then cut it at the bend so the cloth will lay flat and stick to both sides of the turn.

✓ When fiberglass mat is "wet out" with resin, it does not become as transparent as woven cloth, but its color changes sufficiently to indicate that it is saturated; it would be impossible to mistakenly leave mat only partially wet out.

✓ Finish coats of any resin should be flowed on in thin coats (not brushed back and forth).

✓ When cleaning amine blush from cured epoxy, don't use acetone on the rag, and don't use a tack cloth. Moisten the rag with plain water or alcohol.

✓ An epoxy repair can be finished by covering it with release fabric, which is specially treated so epoxy will not adhere to it. Use a spreader over the fabric to smooth the surface of the repair and squeeze out excess resin. This step minimizes sanding. In addition, when the release fabric is removed, the amine blush is also removed.

✓ If a bunch of tiny bubbles appear on the surface of epoxy resin shortly after application, brush across them lightly with a sponge or foam brush. They could be ignored initially, then sanded away later, but that would just leave a bunch of tiny air pockets to fill later, so the smoother the resin each time, the better.

✓ Even a small amount of colloidal silica mixed into epoxy resin will help counteract the tendency of resin to sag down a vertical surface.

✓ When finishing a repair made with tape, it's better to fair out the edges, using a resin and microballoon mix, than to sand off the edge of the fiberglass.

SANDING

Whether the final coat will be gelcoat or paint, the surface must be sanded with a series of fine to finer-grit sandpapers to remove all gloss and sanding scratches from the coarser papers and to ensure a supersmooth coat.

All cured resin is hard to sand, but epoxy and vinylester are specially tough. Start with a finishing sander and good quality paper. (Auto-parts stores or others that sell automotive paint will carry professional grade sandpapers, if the marina does not.) Sanding should start with 80- to 100-grit and work up to 180 or 220 before switching to hand-sanding with wet-or-dry paper. For the glossy finish coat desired on fiberglass surfaces, 320-grit wet-or-dry paper is probably fine enough for final sanding, but some people prefer to continue up to 600 grit. It should be noted that the actual finish coating of gelcoat or paint can later be

A hand block sander is useful on small repairs.

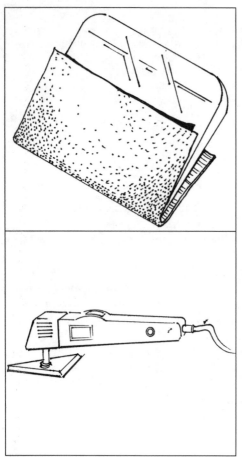

Sandpaper wrapped around a plastic spreader enables the user to maintain a flat surface.

The "mouse" electric sander gets into hard-to-reach places.

fine-sanded with up to 1200 or 1500 grit paper, though few people consider it necessary.

✓ Vibrating finishing sanders stay level; the triangular "mouse" type can get into tight places.

✓ When using wet-or-dry paper, place a small container of water close by so the paper can be dipped and rinsed from time to time. Keep a second piece of paper handy and use one to "scrub" the other. The paper will work better and last longer if the sanding clogs are removed often.

✓ Don't use sandpaper until it shreds. As soon as it requires more effort to do the same amount of work, get a new piece of paper.

✓ A folded piece of sandpaper will NOT produce the desired overall flat surface because it cannot stay level enough. Depressions will form as the sandpaper (and then the sanded surface) reflects the inconsistent pressure from fingers. Better to fold the paper around a plastic spreader or wide putty knife and hold it as flat against the surface as is practical.

✓ A hand-block sander works fairly well to sand down high spots, but it must be used with caution to prevent a dent and wave effect that comes from accidentally tilting the block. To reach narrow spots, wrap sandpaper around a small piece of wood.

FINISH COATS

In boat manufacturing, gelcoat is the first thing into the mold (since it is the top coat when the boat comes out). Though it is a type of polyester resin, gelcoat is more sensitive to temperature and humidity—even fiberglass professionals occasionally have problems with its cure. When it works according to plan, it will provide a durable finish coat for a fiberglass repair, and since it is often possible to color the gelcoat to match the existing surface, many people prefer to use it when the repair has been done with polyester resin. (Although it is possible to use gelcoat over an epoxy repair too, most amateur fiberglass workers choose not to use it.)

Ideally, when finishing with gelcoat, the repaired area should be left a bit low relative to the surrounding surface. The gelcoat is thick; it will top off the patch until it is raised slightly above the existing surface. Then the final sanding will bring the gelcoat down to level out with the surrounding area. Apply gelcoat to small areas with a putty knife; use a brush to paint the gelcoat over larger areas.

After the gelcoat is applied, it should be sprayed with PVA to seal out the air and ensure a cure. An alternative to spraying is to tape a piece of plastic wrap tightly over the entire patch. This not only seals out the air, but also flattens the patch to shorten sanding time. (Finishing gelcoat will cure in air, eliminating the need to cover the patch.)

Once cured, final finishing is done by more sanding (with ever finer-grit papers), followed by the application of rubbing compound or polishing compound. These products resemble a cream wax, but they contain a mild abrasive that helps produce the finest possible finish on the gelcoat. A lamb's wool pad on a buffer can be used with these compounds, or a soft cloth and old-fashioned elbow grease.

✓ If the repaired section is on a vertical plane, then gelcoat may be a best choice for a finish coat. Gelcoat is thicker than regular resin, thus much thicker than paint, so it is less likely to run or drip down the side.

✓ Even though a pigment is theoretically the same color as the boat's gelcoat, the finished patch probably won't match exactly, simply because the old gelcoat is somewhat faded or chalked due to exposure. As time passes, the two will blend visually.

✓ If gelcoat is to be tinted, add pigment to neutral gelcoat.

✓ The color of a tinted gelcoat will look different when it dries. To ensure the closest color match, mix small amounts of colored gelcoat as samples, keeping track of the amount of pigment added per portion of resin. Spread a swatch of each mixture. When they dry, compare them to the existing surface and choose the best match.

✓ Mix resin and catalyst first, then add pigment.

✓ For small repairs, some gelcoat products are formulated to cure without the usual procedure of sealing out air.

If the final coating will be paint, many choices are available. Different brands require different levels of expertise and also fit different budgets. Often mentioned are the professional-grade, high-performance two-part coatings: Awlgrip, Imron, Sherwin-Williams, and others of similar formulation. These are usually applied only by professionals doing complete repaint jobs, seldom by the boatowner on a small repair. These coatings are very expensive, and it is difficult if not impossible to purchase them in small amounts.

Traditional enamels and two-part epoxy paints are still available, but most commonly used today are two-part polyurethane paints, for their toughness and high gloss. These are made for consumer use. They are reasonably easy to use, and readily found at marine stores, along with their recommended primers. Whichever brand is chosen, it is most important to follow the manufacturer's recommendation for the correct primer, particularly for use over new resin. Too much time and work and money is involved to risk a do-over.

Even if an epoxy repair has been pigmented to match the existing surface, the epoxy must be overcoated with paint to protect it from ultraviolet.

Paint can be applied by brushing or spraying—manufacturers provide separate thinners for each method. Brushing demands the use of a good-quality natural bristle brush; badger is still popular. Spraying is relatively simple, using the Preval Paint Sprayer. A small bottle holds the paint and attaches to an aerosol can; it can be found in auto-parts, marine, or hardware stores, and

Tape a piece of plastic tightly over a gelcoat patch to seal out air and allow the gelcoat to cure.

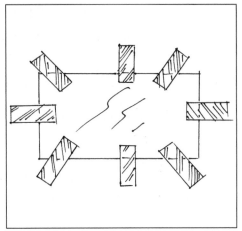

even some home-repair warehouses. Spraying usually results in a much smoother job, assuming the paint-to-thinner ratio is correct and the person wielding the sprayer is careful to keep it moving. Even when a paint overload creates an orange-peel edge or a few dreaded drips, the bad spots can be removed with fine sanding after the paint dries. The spray should be feathered out lightly beyond the repaired patch, so the newly painted spot will blend better with the existing surface.

✓ When choosing the paint, try to get recommendations from people who used the product some time ago. Almost all paint jobs look great immediately after application, but the lasting quality is equally, perhaps more, important.

✓ If an expensive paint will last five years or more, there may be little saving in choosing a cheaper one-or-two-year paint.

✓ Don't thin paint too much in striving for a smooth finish. It may look good initially, but chalk quickly because of a lack of pigment.

✓ While it may seem easier to paint rather than use gelcoat, it may not be quicker. Two products (primer and paint) are involved, and two coats of each could be needed. Each coat will most likely require prior sanding, so total work time will easily be more with the option of paint.

✓ With some paints, a high-build or surfacing primer can be used. This is a thick primer that does more than just prime; it fills any scratches or dents still remaining after sanding the fiberglass. However, using this type of primer means more sanding.

✓ If the repair is below the waterline, read the small print on both paint and primer cans to be sure the products are suitable for that application.

CLEANUP

Brushes used with either type of resin can be cleaned with the traditional three-can step-down process, also using acetone. Rinse the brush in the first can, then the second, and then the third. As the first batch of acetone gets too loaded with goo, remove it; move the bottom two cans up one place and use fresh acetone in the third. Later, if the cans are allowed to sit undisturbed (covered to prevent evaporation), much of the resin will settle and the acetone can be reused. Nevertheless, this is a time-and-acetone-consuming task. Also, since solvent residue may be a source of resin contamination, such cleaning seems even more undesirable. For these reasons, most people use throwaway brushes.

If rollers are being used to apply resin, the actual roller will be removed and tossed, but the handle can and should be cleaned as soon as possible for reuse. Too much later and it may not be possible.

Acetone can be used to clean uncured epoxy from tools, but only if suitable gloves are worn (sturdier gloves than the latex disposables). It is preferable to use isopropyl alcohol or even plain white vinegar, followed by a soap-and-water scrub.

Cleaning resin off hands should not be a consideration—long sleeves and rubber gloves should preclude this situation. However, if it does become necessary due to a glove failure or a forgetful worker, a can of waterless soap will help with the resin removal, and a follow-up soap-and-water wash will help with the residue. Coating hands with a barrier cream before starting any resin work is good prevention.

✓ When wiping surfaces with any solvent, use plain white cotton rags. Otherwise, the work area may develop a pattern of colored streaks, as the dye in either a cloth rag or a paper towel dissolves with the solvent, creating its own contamination and requiring additional cleaning.

✓ If resin spills, it must be cleaned up; it will not evaporate and disappear. Pick up the spill after it has been soaked into sand or dirt. Rags or paper towels could be dangerous when soaked with resin, creating an environment for spontaneous combustion if the resin gets too warm.

✓ If it's possible to collect a quantity of the spilled resin in a container (by scooping it up with a small can or paper cup), mix in a bit of catalyst or hardener so it will eventually cure. It's easier to toss a dirty glass rock than a pile of goo.

✓ Dispose of all empty resin cans according to local regulations. Many marinas and boatyards have specific dumpsters or areas where these items are to be left for pickup by the appropriate waste disposal company.

✓ Uncured epoxy on clothing can be removed, at least partially, with waterless soap. Launder all boatyard work clothes together, separated from the good clothes.

✓ If leftover polyester resin must be stored for a time, the cooler it is kept, the better. If it's in a translucent plastic container, keep it in a dark area. Pour the leftover portion of resin from a large can into a clean, small can.

✓ Epoxy resin and hardener will keep for years if the containers are closed properly and the cans kept at room temperature.

Chapter 5

Touch-ups

*This chapter describes typical surface-coat problems and shows
the steps necessary to make repairs, but chapter 4 can also be
referenced for details on working with the materials.*

Cosmetic or surface touch-ups are subdivided by the type and
depth of the damage, but even minor imperfections should not be
ignored. Gelcoat is the laminate's protective layer; scratches can
and do lead to deeper damage, so early attention can head off
future problems.

OXIDATION

Most noticeable on colored hulls, oxidation causes gelcoat to have a
chalky, faded appearance. The gloss is gone and so is the depth of
color, but if the condition is in its early stages, color and shine can
often be restored fairly easily.

1. Scrub the surface. If it is badly soiled or mildewed, use TSP
   (trisodium phosphate) in the wash water. Rinse and dry.
2. Use a dewaxer to remove all old wax.
3. Apply fiberglass rubbing compound and buff until the color is restored. Buffing can be done by hand if the area is small, or with a
   polisher if the whole hull needs work. Since compounds are available with different abrasives, it is possible to proceed from a
   coarse to a fine polishing compound, if so desired.
4. Apply a coat of wax to protect and help maintain the finish.

✓ Old cotton socks or terrycloth towels are good waxing cloths.

SCUFF MARKS AND VERY LIGHT SCRATCHES

Scuff marks and light scratches can usually be removed with a
light sanding followed by buffing:

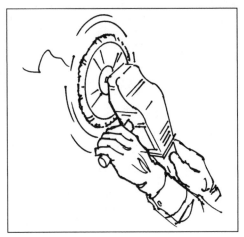

Use polishing compound and a buffer to remove light scratches. The job can be done by hand too; many suggest it will be done better.

1. Clean and dewax, as for oxidation.
2. Tape off the section around the scratch, so sanding is confined to the smallest area. Sand until the scratch is no longer visible, using fine-grit wet paper; how fine a grit depends on each individual's idea of "good enough." Most people stop at 400 or 600.
3. Buff with rubbing compound.
4. Finish with a coat of wax.

✓ Ideal for this very fine surface sanding is a small, slightly flexible block sold at auto-paint stores, available up to 1200 and 1500 grit.

SCRATCHES CONFINED TO GELCOAT

Although it seems that a simple surface filling and sanding would fix scratches, that is often just a temporary fix—the same marks can reappear in a short time. To discourage their return, it is necessary to widen the scratches a bit to provide a broader surface to hold the new gelcoat.

1. Scrape the path of each scratch to widen it. The sharp point of an old-fashioned can opener is a good tool. The corner of a metal putty knife or chisel will work too.
2. Clean the area with the appropriate solvent or water; wipe with a clean rag.
3. Mix gelcoat and apply it with a small plastic putty knife or spreader.

4. Seal the gelcoat to cure it (spray with PVA or tape a piece of plastic wrap over the surface).

5. Next day: if the repair is on the hull or cabin side, sand the cured gelcoat. Start with 120 or 150 paper on a sanding block, then use wet/dry paper moving up in stages to 600 (or finer) without the block.

6. Buff and wax.

   Note: If the repair is on deck in a nonskid area, a supersmooth finish is not essential, since it will be overcoated with textured nonskid.

✓ Gelcoat is sold in a paste form; this thicker formulation is good for scratch repairs.

SPIDER CRACKS (ALSO CALLED CRAZING OR STRESS CRACKS)

A spider-web pattern of cracks in the gelcoat could be the result of an impact (dropping a wrench or a winch handle) or it could indicate an area where the fiberglass laminate is under some stress. This kind of damage is often found on the deck, where stanchions and other hardware are attached. The corners of a cockpit sole are other common sites. The temptation is to treat these cracks the same way as ordinary scratches, and while it may be worth a try, it will probably prove to be a temporary cover-up. A better fix involves redoing the gelcoat.

Stress cracks:
a. Stress cracks indicate an area where the laminate is under some stress, but it may be possible to repair them the same way as surface scratches.

Stress cracks:
b. Scrape over each crack with a sharp-pointed tool to widen the patching surface.

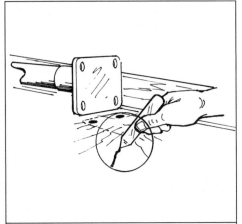

c. Apply new gelcoat with a putty knife or plastic spreader.

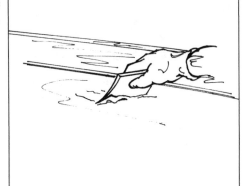

d. When the gelcoat is cured, sand the surface flush with the surrounding area.

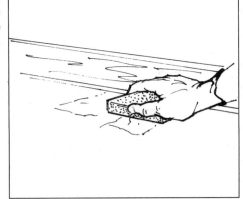

1. Clean the surface around the cracks.
2. Sand the area with coarse to medium paper on a disk sander to remove the gelcoat.
3. Clear the dust away, clean the surface.
4. Apply new gelcoat with plastic putty knife or spreader.
5. Seal the gelcoat from air so it cures.
6. Sand to 600 or further and finish the job to match the existing surface (buff and wax smooth areas, apply nonskid for decks).

✓ Two-part polyurethane paint is an alternative to gelcoat; it must be applied over the appropriate primer. This option would be especially practical if the entire surrounding area is in need of a new surface coat.

✓ For a temporary patch of a small area of nonskid, mix nonskid granules into paint. Even though this does not match the deck's molded-in pattern, the patched section will be clean and safe until a more permanent patch can be fabricated.

✓ If the crazing pattern returns, the fiberglass structure in the area must be strengthened to prevent the flexing that is causing the cracks. See chapter 9, "Stiffeners."

BADLY DETERIORATED GELCOAT

This condition is frequently found on older boats. Early fiberglass boats were generally overbuilt, and apparently the same construction theory often applied to the gelcoat, resulting in overly thick and overly brittle gelcoat. The surface shows an overall pattern of deep crazing. Big chips of gelcoat may already be gone, exposing the fiberglass laminate beneath. Some people try to "glue"

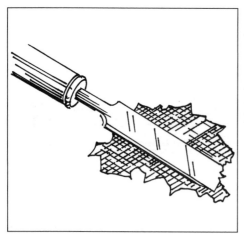

Deteriorated gelcoat:
a. Deteriorated gelcoat shows an overall pattern of deep cracks. Some pieces of the gelcoat may have chipped away. Remove all loose pieces with a chisel.

Deteriorated gelcoat:
b. Sand the remaining surface and grind a clean, beveled edge on the repair area with a burr tip on a rotary tool.

c. Apply new gelcoat with a plastic spreader.

d. Sand the gelcoat level with the surrounding area.

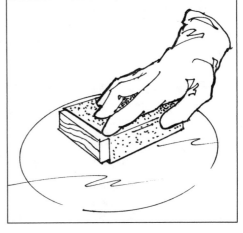

the cracked surface in place with epoxy resin (hoping it will seep between the cracks) or a thick primer (hoping it will span the cracks), but neither method works—they succeed only in a short-term cover-up. The permanent repair starts with removing all the gelcoat.

1. With a disk sander and coarse paper, remove all gelcoat down to clean fiberglass laminate. If the damage is confined to a small section, round the repair area and bevel the edge.
2. Clear the surface of sanding dust and wipe with alcohol.
3. Apply new gelcoat.
4. Seal the gelcoat to cure it.
5. Sand and finish the job to match the existing surface (buff and wax smooth surfaces, apply nonskid for decks).

AIR BUBBLES (VOIDS)

During the initial lay-up, voids may be created—small spots where the resin-saturated cloth did not adhere to the gelcoat in the mold. Corners are probable sites; the gelcoat spans the void so the problem is not visible initially, but eventually the thin surface breaks away, exposing the gap beneath. These are easy to fix:

1. Clean the surface around the void.
2. Scrape out bits of the top coat and any loose fibers, and sand the edges of the area either by hand or with a burr tip on a small rotary tool, like a Dremel.
3. Clean the inside thoroughly.
4. If the hole is small, fill it with polyester putty. To fill a larger hole, it may be desirable to add some reinforcement to the putty, like bits of chopped strand fiberglass (the patch will be less brittle with the glass). Fill the hole in two or three applications, rather than all at once.
5. Sand (use a hand-block sander), add more putty if necessary to build up the shape to match the surrounding surface, and sand again.
6. Top with gelcoat, seal it, and when cured, buff the patch.

DEEP SCRATCHES, NICKS, DENTS, GOUGES

Damage that reaches beyond the gelcoat requires more attention. Whether dealing with a deep ding or a ragged gouge, the problem extends into the laminate and so must the repair. This can be done with either polyester or epoxy resin—only the finishing steps will change.

To repair a gouge with polyester resin, follow these steps:

1. Clean the area thoroughly.
2. Remove all loose chips and bits of fiber. Expand the area to a round or oval shape and bevel the edge. Sand the exposed fiberglass with 60-grit paper to roughen the surface so it will accept the new repair materials.
3. Clear away sanding dust; wash the surface.
4. If the damage is deep enough to warrant it, cut small fabric patches (as many as needed to build up the desired thickness). Saturate them with resin as they are placed one by one.
5. Leave the thickness of the repair layers slightly low to allow room for top coat.
6. Apply gelcoat and seal the patch with plastic wrap.
7. Finish as usual: fine sand, buff, wax if appropriate.

If the repair is done with epoxy resin instead of polyester, use the following alternate steps:

6. (alternate). After the fabric patches have cured, mix some fairing putty and level out the area. It may take two or three applications, sanding between, to get a perfectly smooth, level surface.
7. Sand in stages up to 320-grit paper.
8. Apply primer and paint, buff if desired, and wax.

COVERING A LARGE SURFACE

A thin covering of fiberglass cloth is often used to protect wood (old or new) and also to provide a whole new surface over a larger fiberglass repair. The job is usually done with one or two layers of 10-ounce cloth.

As with small repairs, fabric pieces should be cut and ready before mixing resin. In some instances, it may be necessary to tape one side of the cloth to the surface to keep it in place while applying the resin. The resin should be mixed and poured in workable batches, and spread onto the cloth with a plastic spreader or roller, followed by a final pass with a metal grooved roller. Obviously, two people working on the project would make the job easier, one mixing and one applying the resin. The cloth turns transparent when it wets out.

If it is necessary to use two pieces of cloth for one layer, the second piece should overlap the first by about one inch. When the resin has cured to "thumb-nail soft," the doubled fabric must be trimmed by cutting through both layers in the center of the overlap, using a sharp mat knife or a plain, single-edged razor blade. The cut ends of both pieces of fabric are then removed, and extra resin is added, if necessary, to "glue" the edges back in place. The two pieces of cloth will now meet at the cut line, with no raised overlap.

A second layer of cloth can be laminated, if desired. Later, additional coats of resin should be applied to fill the weave and provide a protective cover for the fabric.

✓ If the area to be covered curves in places, it may be necessary to cut a slit in the cloth (using sharp scissors) and overlap a section to allow the rest of the cloth to lay flat. This overlap area can be trimmed the same way as the double layer of fabric; cut through both layers with a sharp blade, and remove the cutaway portions.

Chapter 6

Holes

This chapter describes typical problems involving holes in and through fiberglass laminates and shows the steps necessary to make repairs, but chapter 4 can also be referenced for details on working with the materials.

Fixing holes covers a lot of territory—a no-longer-needed screw hole, the neat circular void left by removal of a through-hull fitting or an I/O lower unit, or a jagged section of the hull that indicates a collision with a piling or rock.

SCREW HOLES

Whether fixing a stripped screw hole or filling the holes left after a stanchion or cleat was removed, the procedure is the same:

1. Clean out the hole and also clean a small circle of the surrounding surface. Scrape out caulking; drill the hole a bit bigger if necessary to guarantee a clean edge throughout.
2. Bevel the edge around the top of the hole (so the patch is more likely to hold and not shrink away from a tiny gap).
3. If the hole is completely through the hull or deck, block the inside or bottom surface. Put a small piece of plastic directly under the hole (because epoxy won't stick to plastic), then tape over and around the plastic to hold it as tightly as possible.
4. Use a small artist's brush to paint the inside of the hole with epoxy resin.
5. Thicken epoxy resin with colloidal silica, leaving it sufficiently liquid so it will drip or drain downward, and dab it into the hole. This dabbing procedure will probably require more than one application, as the resin will drip down to the bottom very slowly.
6. When the hole is filled, allow the resin to cure.

7. Remove the tape and plastic from the bottom; fill and sand as needed to level the epoxy patch with the surrounding surfaces at top and bottom.

8. Retouch the top surface with paint or gelcoat as desired. (Gelcoat can be used over small epoxy repairs without special preparation—a thorough sanding and cleaning will suffice.)

✓ Instead of filling the hole to the top with the resin mix, use a white epoxy patching putty for the last $\frac{1}{8}$-inch or so. If the surrounding surface is white, then spot-painting may not be necessary.

✓ Don't try to push thick patching putty into a deep screw hole. It will always leave an air bubble, sometimes visible, sometimes not, but either way the repair has a hollow spot.

✓ A syringe could be used to inject epoxy into the hole.

✓ Clean up excess epoxy putty before it cures. It is much easier to scrape away soft putty than to sand cured epoxy.

GOUGE (TORN EDGE)

If the hull lost the battle with a large bolt on a bollard, or, worse, a large rock near the shoreline, the resulting scratch can be very deep.

1. Clear away all loose pieces and fibers, clean the surface area, then grind the edges to a uniform bevel and a smoother, more round or oblong shape.

2. Clear the dust and clean the surface again.

3. Cut pieces of fiberglass fabric (or alternate fabric and mat) to fit the gap.

4. Saturate and layer three or four pieces of fiberglass, then wait for a partial cure before adding more, if more are required.

5. If working with polyester resin, leave the patch slightly low, to be filled with the gelcoat layer. Apply gelcoat and seal the patch until it cures. If working with epoxy resin, finish the patch with thickened putty for an even surface.

6. If gelcoat, sand, clean, buff, and wax if appropriate. If epoxy, sand, clean, prime, and paint.

✓ When fixing small patches, protect the surfaces near the work area by taping paper over all but the repair section. Or, wax the area first; anything that spills will be easier to remove.

Gouge: a. A deep gouge should be repaired with cloth and resin to provide strength as well as fill the gap.

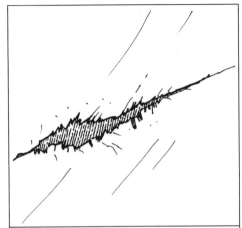

b. Grind the surface and expand the edges to create a clean, rounded or oblong shape. Apply layers of resin-saturated cloth to fill.

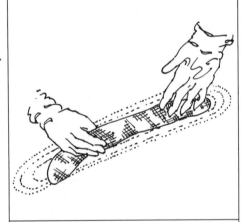

c. Use a putty knife to spread gelcoat over the repair.

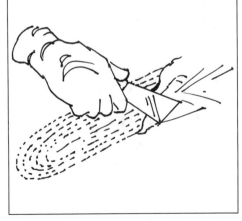

SMALL HOLE IN NONSTRUCTURAL AREA

An instrument has been removed, so there's no need for the gauge anymore. Now there's a 2-inch hole in the plywood-cored bulkhead waiting for a quick repair.

1. Clean both sides of the bulkhead.
2. Sand the surface on both sides a few inches beyond the hole.
3. Cut a circle of wood slightly smaller than the diameter of the hole. The wood should be slightly thinner than the bulkhead, to allow the addition of some fiberglass fabric on each side.
4. Set the wood plug in place with thick putty.
5. When that putty cures, use more to fill in all the gaps on both sides.
6. Add a layer or two of fabric on both sides, and coat with extra resin to smooth out the surfaces on both sides.
7. If using polyester resin, finish with gelcoat, buff, and wax. If using epoxy, use thickened resin to level both surfaces, sand, prime, and paint.

✓ If using polyester resin and thickener to make putty, be sure to use finishing resin.

HOLE THROUGH THE HULL

Patching a hole in the hull, especially one below the waterline, may be the most critical repair a person will make. This is the area where a good bond between new and old material is most impor-

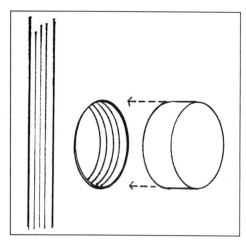

Hole in nonstructural area: Use a wooden plug to fill most of a hole in a nonstructural area. Fill gaps with putty and top with fabric pieces.

tant. It is desirable to increase the area of the bonding surface, and this is done by tapering the edge of the hole. The taper or bevel is expressed as a ratio, most commonly recommended as 12:1 (width of bevel to thickness of laminate). A ¼-inch thickness would thus dictate a 3-inch bevel; a ½-inch thickness, a 6-inch bevel; and so on.

Because any repair is a secondary bond, and because of the location of this repair, epoxy is generally considered to be the better choice: it has better adhesive properties, and it does not shrink like polyester might.

Holes can be patched using multiple layers of fiberglass cloth or alternate layers of cloth and mat (start and end with mat). Another possibility is biaxial fabric with mat. This will build a thickness fast

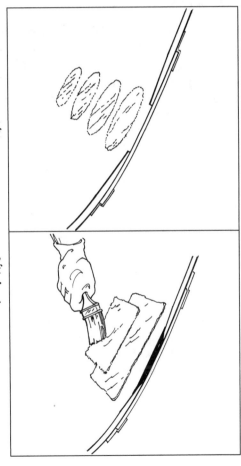

Hole through hull:
a. When the back side is accessible, patch a hole from the inside. Tape a backing plate to the outer surface; grind the inside edge to a 12:1 bevel, and laminate layers of fiberglass.

b. When the patch is filled, apply two or three pieces of fiberglass fabric to cover the patched hole.

and provide a strong patch for a hole below the waterline, but the thicker fabric will be more difficult to saturate.

When cutting fabric to repair the beveled hole, the pieces will vary in size, each slightly larger than the last as the bevel increases the diameter of the area to be filled. While it may seem most logical to place the fabric in a small-to-large order (matching the shape of the hole), in fact, many repairs are done by placing them large to small. Either way is acceptable—the end result is the same as far as filling the gap. One reason for placing the largest piece of fabric in first is that it will span the entire repair area and provide a strong base, rather than bonding only one edge at a time. In addition, there is less chance for individual pieces of cloth to crimp at the edges and create voids or pockets of solid resin instead of resin-saturated fabric.

Back Side Accessible

When the hole is completely through the hull and the inside of the damaged area is accessible, it's most practical to patch the hole from the inside. That way, the bevel will be on the inside surface, so the exterior finished surface will have the smallest patch. Also, more pieces of cloth can be used in covering layers over the patch.

1. Clean the surfaces on both sides.
2. From the inside, grind the edges to the desired 12:1 bevel, and sand the surface area out about 4 inches.
3. On the outside, tape a piece of plastic sheeting against the surface, reaching past the gap by about an inch all around. Then put a fairly stiff piece of cardboard over the plastic and tape or otherwise brace it securely to act as a backing plate for the repair. (The cardboard could be wrapped with the plastic first, then taped—whichever method results in the tightest fit against the outside hull surface.)
4. Cut the fabric pieces.
5. Mix resin and saturate each layer of fabric in place. Use a grooved roller to squeeze out air bubbles and excess resin. Place three or four plies at a time, then allow a partial cure before adding the next group of fabric layers. If necessary, scrape or sand off any bits of fiber or resin lumps that are raised so they don't interfere with the bonding of the next group of fabric layers.
6. When the patch is complete, allow it to cure.
7. Use a putty mixture to level out dents.
8. Sand smooth.

9. On the inside surface, cover the entire patch area with two or three pieces of fabric that extend about 3 inches beyond the repair. With resin and putty, fair out the edges of the cloth into the surrounding surface. Since this is the inside hull surface, it is probably not usually visible, and so a perfect finish coat is not necessary. Leave as is or finish as desired.

10. To complete the outside hull repair, remove the backing plate. The patch will probably be a bit high, since the backing plate cannot stay perfectly flush with the outer surface. Hand sand the surface to level it out; use putty to fill any voids and smooth out the surface, sanding between applications.

11. Sand to 320, clean, apply finish coat of primer and paint.

✓ Other materials that are flexible enough to use as a backing plate include ⅛" paneling, a sheet of acrylic, or mahogany doorskin.

Back Side Not Accessible

Even when the back side of a hole is not accessible, a backing plate must be positioned. In this case, the backing plate will be attached to the inner surface of the hull, and it will become part of the permanent repair.

1. Clean the outside surface.
2. Bevel the edge of the hole and clean again.

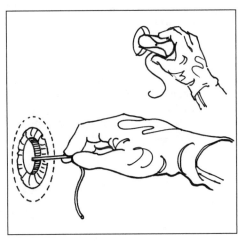

Back side not accessible: Bend the backing patch and push it through the hole. Spread quick-setting epoxy on the inside surface, put the backing patch in place, and pull it tightly against inner surface.

3. Reach through the hole to clean and rough sand (60-grit) the inside surface about an inch beyond the hole.

4. Make a fabric patch to serve as a backing plate. Cut two or three pieces of fiberglass fabric sized to be about an inch larger than the hole all around; saturate them with epoxy resin, and "layer" them together on top of a piece of plastic, so the cured patch can be moved easily. Once cured, this patch will be flexible enough to bend slightly.

5. In order to hold the patch while it is being placed in position, put two small screws into the patch, leaving the heads raised to form mini-handles. Tie a string around one of the screw heads, for retrieval if the patch should fall.

6. Mix some thick putty, using colloidal silica. Reach through the hole, and slather a one-inch strip of putty on the inside surface around the hole. Also spread putty on the outer circle of the patch, where it will touch the back side surface.

7. Bend the patch slightly and push it through the hole; turn it to its proper alignment (if the hole is oval instead of round) and pull it taut against the back. Secure it until the putty cures. Scrape away excess putty that squeezes out onto the front surface of the backing plate. Five-minute epoxy would be a good product to use here.

8. When the epoxy cures, remove the screws and sand off any remaining putty blobs.

9. Cut fabric pieces.

10. Build up the patch thickness with resin-saturated fabric. Place three or four layers at a time, then allow partial curing before applying more fabric.

11. Add extra topcoats of resin, fill imperfections with putty, use release fabric, if desired. Allow to cure. Wash to remove amine blush (if necessary) and prepare surface for finish coating: sand, prime, and paint.

✓ Although it seems that fine sanding dust would be absorbed in resin, too much of it could act as a release agent instead, preventing a good bond. When sanding between layers, be sure the surface is dust free before adding more plies.

✓ After cleaning surfaces, do not touch! A gloved hand can transfer whatever's on the glove from the last use, and an ungloved hand—though it should not even be a consideration—can leave an oily residue that will affect adhesion of the resin.

KEEL GOUGES

Though not actually a hole, a gouge in the bottom of the keel is the kind of repair that requires the same kind of serious attention.

Usually caused by a firm grounding, a deep scrape or gouge in the keel can open the composite to water intrusion, which becomes an ongoing source of deterioration to the fiberglass.

Ideally, the boat should be checked when it is hauled and still in the sling. Once it has been blocked, it may be impossible to see the problem, much less repair it.

If the boat can be blocked farther off the ground than usual, it should be possible to do some repair work. Clean off the bottom paint and sand or scrape as much of the damaged surface as is necessary to expose the extent of damage. As with other repairs, it is smart to widen the area where the new materials will bond.

✓ If there's not enough room for a disk grinder, a rotary tool might work. Failing that, use chisels, rasps, round files, and coarse sandpaper until solid fiberglass is reached.

✓ If the boat can't be blocked higher, it might be possible to dig a hole under the section that needs work. But ask the yard manager before digging!

Once the damaged section has a clean edge, let the boat dry out. How long this may take is an unknown. Watch it to see if water is draining. If a brown-colored liquid is draining, that may be a sign of disintegration within the laminate; more of the surrounding area should be removed.

With luck, the draining will cease quickly, the hull will be dry, and patching can be done.

1. Give the area one final cleaning.
2. Cut strips of fiberglass cloth to fit the gap.
3. Paint a coat of epoxy resin on the sanded edges, then layer the cloth pieces into the gap, saturating each with more epoxy.
4. When patch is level with surface, allow it to cure.
5. Use thick putty (made with colloidal silica and milled fibers, not microballoons) to fair the patch.
6. Put two or three layers of fabric over the patched area, extending past the limits of the patch by a couple of inches. Fair this into the existing surface with more thickened resin. This section will remain a high spot, but better that than a weeping laminate.

Chapter 7

Cores

*This chapter describes typical problems with core construction and
shows the steps necessary to make repairs, but chapter 4 can also
be referenced for details on working with the materials.*

In core or sandwich construction, some type of core material is
sandwiched between two skins of fiberglass. With this type of construction, the fiberglass skins provide the strength while the core provides the stiffness, the end result being a strong but lightweight hull.

Plywood was the original core material, but in today's boats,
the most commonly used core is end-grain balsa. This material is
made up of small squares of balsa wood held together by a light
fabric, so that it remains flexible enough to adapt to boat shapes.
Synthetic "closed-cell" rigid foam is also used as core, made of
either polyurethane or polyvinyl chloride; these do not absorb water. Other types, like a honeycomb-patterned material, are available for special applications but are not used for ordinary repairs.

Even if a boat has a solid fiberglass hull, its deck may be cored;
consequently, repairs involving sandwich construction are common. While a deck may not show any visible sign of damage, it
may feel slightly soft or "spongy" in spots. It might even squish a
little underfoot, a definite indication of trouble. Any place a screw
goes into the deck, the potential for water intrusion exists. Perhaps the core separated from one or both of the skins, because of
poor adhesion initially or because some impact forced the skin to
shear. Whatever the reason, the deck needs to be fixed.

The first step is to determine the boundaries of the damage.
This can be done easily by tapping the deck with the handle of a
chisel or screwdriver and listening for the difference in sound that
will indicate the extent of the damaged area. Though sounds are
hard to describe clearly in words, the comparison between good
and bad will be noticeable—the damaged area will sound more
hollow, or flat, than the solid deck area. (One person described the
good deck sound as a ring, and the bad deck sound as a thunk.)

Once the area has been identified, a few holes should be drilled into (but not completely through) the core. The material that backs out with the drill will show if the core is wet or damaged (bits of soft or rotten wood fibers may be seen, or pieces of powdery or crumbled foam). These conditions will direct the required repair.

Because core repairs require good adhesion and involve the additional material of the core itself, the use of epoxy is strongly recommended.

DELAMINATED CORE (DECK)

If the core is dry but the top skin has separated, the fix is easy.

1. Drill a grid of holes in the area about 1 inch apart.
2. Vacuum the holes and apply heat with a heat gun or hair dryer, just in case some trace of dampness remains inside.
3. Mix epoxy resin with hardener, thicken with colloidal silica to ketchup consistency, and fill the holes, using a syringe to force the epoxy into the holes and under the skin. Cut the tip of the syringe at an angle to help direct the epoxy into the space under the skin.
4. Place a piece of plastic across the top of the repair area.
5. Put weights on top of the deck—cement blocks, bricks, even a 5-gallon water bottle. The epoxy should spread into the space between the core and the skin, reattaching the skin as it seals the holes.
6. When the epoxy has cured, finish the surface to blend with the surrounding area.

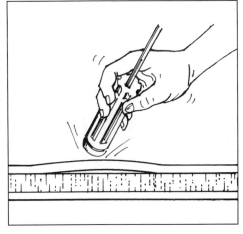

Delaminated core:
a. To locate the boundary of core delamination, tap the surface with the handle of a screwdriver or chisel, and listen for the difference in sound between the solid area and the delaminated section.

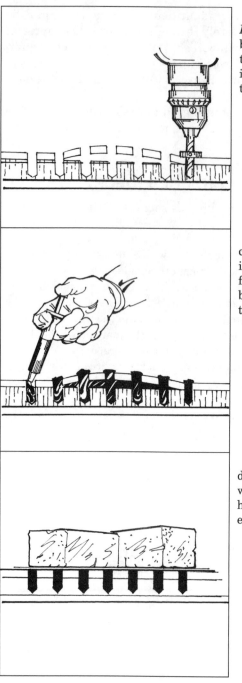

Delaminated core:
b. Drill a series of holes through the top skin and into, but not through, the core.

c. Inject thickened epoxy into the holes; also try to force it into the space between the top skin and the core.

d. Weigh down the area with bricks or other heavy items until the epoxy cures.

WET CORE (DECK)

If the core shows that it is still wet but seems to be otherwise intact (no crushed section, no crumbling, no rot), it may be possible to dry it out and repair it the same way as for a delaminated core.

1. Drill a number of holes in a grid pattern about 1 inch apart.
2. Use a wet/dry vacuum to remove as much water as possible.
3. Use a heat gun or hair dryer to hurry the drying process.
4. When dry, proceed as for delaminated core: inject thickened epoxy, weigh down the skin, finish to match existing surface.

Wet core: a. When core is wet, drill holes into but not all the way through the core. Remove as much water as possible with wet/dry vacuum.

b. Use a heat gun or hair dryer to help dry the core.

Wet core: c. Inject thickened epoxy resin to fill the holes and reattach any sections of core that have separated from the skins.

✓ To speed the process of drying a core, drill a few holes completely through the bottom skin too (but expect to hear arguments from others in the boatyard). Water will drain out the bottom holes faster than it will evaporate out the top. Of course, the holes must be properly filled later with thickened epoxy so this does create an additional step.

DAMAGED CORE (DECK)

If the core structure appears to be damaged beyond repair (wood core is rotted, foam is crushed or crumbled from an impact), it must be replaced.

1. Sound the surrounding deck in order to establish the boundaries of the area that needs to be removed; square off the section and extend it past the actual damaged area.
2. With a router, cut through the top skin and remove it. (Most of it will probably already be unattached from the core; chisel the rest as necessary.) On all sides, measure a few inches in from the first cut, set the router for the depth of the core, and cut the core on the inner line. (This way, the entire repair will not be done along the same vertical line.)
3. Remove the core. This may require cutting or chiseling, since some of the core will still adhere to the bottom skin. While removing the core, try not to damage the bottom skin beyond unavoidable scratches.

Damaged core: a. Where core is damaged, first remove the top skin, then remove a slightly smaller section of core (so that all repair will not be done along the same vertical line).

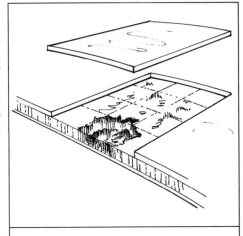

b. Place new piece of core onto bottom skin. To facilitate bonding, use thickened epoxy or a piece of resin-saturated mat between the core and the bottom skin.

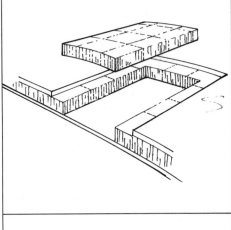

c. After top skin has been replaced, sand both sides of seams to a wide V. Cover the seams with strips of cloth until surface is level.

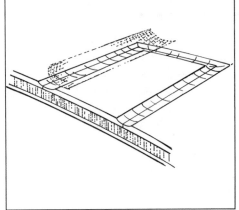

4. Cut a piece of new core material to match the shape of the old, and set it aside. It is generally recommended to use the same type of material, if possible.

5. Sand and clean the bottom skin.

6. If a new top skin is to be laminated, a piece of fiberglass mat can be added between the bottom skin and the core. Cut the mat to fit the hole, saturate it with resin, place the core, and weigh it down until the resin cures. The mat helps to form a good bond between the core and the bottom skin, but if the original top skin is to be replaced, an added layer of mat could raise the patch above the surrounding surface, requiring some creative fairing.

7. If mat is not used, coat the bottom skin with epoxy resin thickened with colloidal silica to ketchup consistency. Then place the core piece and weigh it down until the putty cures.

8. Fill the gaps around all sides of the core with thickened putty. Smooth out the putty along the top of the seams so it does not interfere with replacement of the top skin.

9. If the top skin was removed intact, replace it, using thickened resin between the core and the skin. If the top skin is not reusable, cut fabric and mat pieces and make a new top skin.

10. To ensure the best possible reconnection of the top skin, as well as to prevent a future crack at the place of joining, sand both sides of the seam (between the portion of top skin that was just replaced and the existing top surface) to a V bevel. Then fill the indentation with fabric strips and resin.

DAMAGED CORE (HULL)

If core damage is found in the boat hull, the problem may be more than the amateur fiberglass worker wants to tackle. If the damage occurred some time ago, then water absorption may have been ongoing for all that time. It will be necessary to check a large area of the hull for moisture, and the repair may prove to be a major undertaking. If, however, the damage was recent and the problem is obvious and confined to the area of impact, it is possible to do the repair following the same procedures as shown for a comparable deck repair.

If the impact holed the exterior skin, obviously the repair must be made from outside, replacing the core and the outer skin.

If the impact resulted in a core delamination but the outer skin is still intact, it may be possible (and it would be desirable) to do the repair from inside. Either way, the same steps apply; only the surface finishing details would differ.

THROUGH-CORE THROUGH-HULL FITTINGS

Any place that water has a chance to sneak into a boat, it will do so. Through-hull fittings are necessary installations, but if the hull is a sandwich construction, extra care must be taken to ensure the core does not invite water ingress.

Wherever a fitting goes through the hull, the hull portion immediately surrounding the fitting should be made solid. Core material should be cut back, and the section filled with "peanut-butter" epoxy putty, thickened and strengthened with milled fibers and colloidal silica.

✓ When replacing a section of core, the usual suggestion is to use the same material for the new piece because this guarantees that old and new core will have the exact same characteristics. However, there can be exceptions. A different material can be used as long as the alternate has the same (or very similar) density as the old material, so the new deck section will have the same strength or resistance as the original. If the densities are noticeably different, a crack would soon be visible at the place where the two cores connect, because one would flex or compress and the other would not.

✓ A different kind of core could be an advantage. If replacing plywood with non-absorbing foam, there can be no future risk of rot. A foam core would be lighter in weight than plywood too.

✓ Replacement core must naturally be the same thickness as the original material. Core is sold in thicknesses ranging from ¼ inch to about 1½ inches.

✓ When finished with a core repair, tap the area again. If all taps sound the same, that's a good sign!

Chapter 8

Blisters

This chapter describes blister problems and shows the steps necessary to make repairs, but chapter 4 can also be referenced for details on working with the materials.

For years after its introduction to marine manufacturing, fiberglass seemed the miracle material: no rot, no rust, easy maintenance. Then came the blister problem. On polyester-based fiberglass hulls everywhere, bubbles began to appear on the underwater section of the hull. Sometimes only a few isolated blisters of varying size would be seen, and other times hundreds of tiny ones would cover the entire hull, prompting the description of "boat pox." After a lot of discussion and study, the probable cause of the problem was determined, though the best method of repair is still a matter of opinion.

It is generally accepted that blistering starts because water from outside has permeated the gelcoat. The water then dissolves certain materials that have been trapped in the laminate since construction, and the combined acidic liquid accumulates in small voids between the gelcoat and the laminate. As more water is brought to these voids, the pressure eventually forces the formation of blisters. The process by which the water is brought into the voids is called osmosis, so the problem is sometimes referred to as "osmotic blistering."

When blisters are broken, an acrid smell confirms that the liquid inside is not plain water. Sometimes, it is even more obvious, as the fluid leaking from the blister is a dark brown color. If the condition is left untreated, this fluid will continue to break down the resin within the hull, causing the fiberglass to delaminate, thus compromising the strength of the hull. This process is called hydrolysis, and it is the more serious problem.

Though these processes are understood, the factors that trigger them are less clear. Blistering seems to be more prevalent on boats kept in warm climates—higher temperature allows more water to permeate the gelcoat and it accelerates the rate of hydrolysis where it has already begun. In addition, these boats are in the water year round. Water inside the boat may also increase the likelihood of blister formation, another reason to keep the bilge dry.

Other factors considered involve questionable workmanship or practices during construction: improper mixing of resin, wrong additives or too many additives, variables of temperature and humidity at the time of laminating.

It is generally agreed that blisters cannot be ignored, but debate continues on the best way to repair blister damage and protect the hull against a reoccurrence. The "easy" fix involves opening and cleaning the blisters, filling and sanding the cavities, then overcoating the repaired spots with epoxy resin to protect those areas against future water intrusion. The more complete fix is to remove the gelcoat entirely, patch any remaining blisters, and cover the entire underwater portion of the hull with a multiple-layer barrier coat of epoxy to prevent the reoccurrence.

SPOT-FIX THE BLISTERS

If the blisters are few and random, it is possible to repair only those areas. Many people consider blister-filling to be just one more aspect of annual maintenance.

1. Pressure wash the hull, then remove the bottom paint a few inches around all affected areas. Use a chemical stripper to remove the bottom paint to prevent paint chips or residue from being forced into the blister cavities or deeper into the laminate.
2. Using a small knife or screwdriver or chisel, pop open the blisters (wear goggles to protect eyes from the blister fluid).
3. Clean out all loose material inside the blisters, let the liquid drain, then wash with water.
4. When dry, grind/sand the blister cavities as deep as necessary until the area all around shows solid fiberglass. If brownish water continues to drain from any cavity, grind deeper into the laminate and allow to drain again.
5. Once it seems that all the bad liquid is out, let the hull dry. How long that will take is another subject of debate, but the time is only a small part of the problem. If blisters are shallow and heat were applied to hurry the process, it could be that a week or two would be long enough, but there is no sure way to know when or whether the hull is really dry. Moisture meters are used to check for

changes in a given area, but they do not "read" the amount of moisture in a boat hull. One of the main concerns about blisters is that if blister fluid is still trapped inside the laminate, then a barrier coat could seal it inside.

6. Assuming no dampness is detected for some time, proceed with filling the blister cavities. Paint the exposed surface with epoxy resin, then fill the cavities with a thickened epoxy, applied in stages, if the cavity is deep.

7. When filled, sand the patches level with the surrounding surface. Add a coat or two of epoxy resin over the repaired areas, to protect against future water absorption.

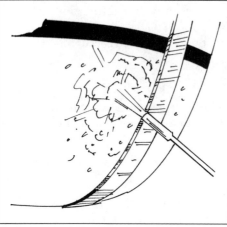

Spot-fix blisters:
a. Pressure-wash the hull as soon as the boat is hauled, and check immediately for blistering. If the bottom is allowed to dry, some blisters may "flatten."

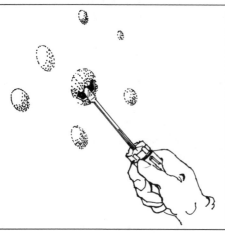

b. Use a small knife, a screwdriver, or a chisel to break open the blisters. Scrape out all loose particles.

The boatowner who chooses the spot-fix option should watch the hull carefully and make written notes, if need be, to compare each year's blister crop with previous years. In this way, it will be clear if the problem is getting worse, which may suggest a different course of action.

FIX THE WHOLE HULL

The more complete blister repair involves removing the gelcoat entirely, fixing any remaining blisters, then coating the underwater portion of the hull with a number of coats of epoxy, which will act as a barrier coat to prevent a reoccurrence of blistering. While much of this can be done by the owner/worker, it cannot be done quickly.

Spot-fix blisters:
c. With a burr bit on drill or rotary tool, grind away all damaged parts of the gelcoat and as far into the laminate as necessary until the surrounding area is solid fiberglass.

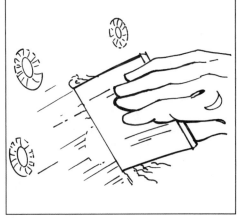

d. When hull is dry, fill all cavities with epoxy thickened with colloidal silica. Microballoons should not be used for this purpose. Milled fibers may be added to the putty for strength.

✓ Though moisture meters do not provide a reading of the amount of moisture in a boat hull, they do note changes. The bottom paint should be removed from the areas of the hull that will be tested. The meter is used to check these areas at regular time intervals, and the owner can see if the readings indicate that the hull is drying. If it is, the readings will eventually reach a level that is "acceptable" for repair work to begin.

✓ Moisture in the hull can be monitored another way. Remove the bottom paint from a number of one-foot-square sections, and tape a small piece of clear plastic onto the hull at each of these places. Seal the edges completely with tape. Moisture will condense inside the plastic. Every few days, remove the plastic, dry it and the hull, and retape the plastic in place. As the hull dries, less moisture will be visible.

Besides the actual work time, drying time must be taken into account, and that can be a huge variable, dependent on the extent of the problem as well as weather conditions. The fortunate few who can store the boat inside have the opportunity to hurry the drying with heaters, and this is a possibility even when stored outside if the yard permits a "tent-over" to hold the heat.

The full repair starts with cleaning the hull, and that includes removal of the bottom paint (use a chemical stripper to avoid grinding paint into blisters). While it is tempting to consider removing paint and gelcoat in one sandblast session, this procedure could also force bits of paint into the blister cavities and into the exposed laminate, and this would interfere with proper bonding of the repair materials.

1. Remove all bottom paint, using a chemical stripper.
2. Remove the gelcoat. This can be done by sanding, sandblasting, or power-planing. Sanding should be done with coarse (36-grit) paper on a disk sander. Blasting must be done with care by a professional or the blister cavities will become the easy part of a larger repair—the hull may be left with thousands of tiny pinholes to be filled, as the pattern of fiberglass weave is exposed. Power-planing is also a "professional-only" job. In this situation, the entire gelcoat (and perhaps a layer or two of laminate, depending on the depth of the damage) is literally planed off.
3. Check all blister cavities, clean them out, and grind away as much additional laminate as is necessary to reach solid fiberglass.
4. Wash the hull, let it dry. Watch it for a few days to see if any blister cavities continue to drain. If so, grind deeper into the laminate

to expose more surface. When it seems that all cavities have stopped draining, leave the boat to dry out completely. If this project can be scheduled to coincide with annual haulout time, the boat might sit for months.

5. When it's time to finish the repair, wash the hull again.

6. Fill the blister cavities. First, coat the surface in each cavity with epoxy resin, being especially careful to wet out any exposed fiberglass showing in the cavities. While the initial coat of resin is still tacky, mix more resin with colloidal silica to a peanut-butter consistency, and use a putty knife to fill the holes, being very careful not to leave air pockets in the putty. For larger cavities, filling may take two or three applications, probably with some sanding between layers. To add some strength to the patches, add some milled fibers to the putty in the larger cavities. The holes should be filled a bit higher than the surrounding surface, to allow leveling out with the final sanding. Excess putty around the holes should be scraped away before it cures.

7. When all patch areas are smooth and level, sand the entire hull with 60-grit paper on a finishing sander.

8. Wash to remove all sanding dust, and let the hull dry thoroughly.

9. Apply the barrier coat. With a foam roller, apply three or four thin coats of epoxy resin, allowing each to cure to tacky stage before applying the next. (Try to avoid drips and bubbles—follow the roller with a foam brush to "tip out" these imperfections before the resin cures.) This may mean waiting two or three hours between coats, even with a fast hardener. If a new coat is applied within two days, it's not necessary to sand the previous coat, but if more time has passed, wash the surface with water and a scrub pad to remove amine blush, and sand lightly before applying the next coat.

✓ For the epoxy barrier coat, add large roller trays to the materials list—the disposable paper liners used with an aluminum tray are practical.

✓ After applying the barrier coats of epoxy, remove the tape masking the boundary before the resin cures; otherwise, it will be difficult to remove at all.

✓ When molding new boats, some manufacturers use vinylester resin for the layer closest to the gelcoat because it is a more effective moisture barrier than standard polyester. If vinylester were an option for repair work, then the putty mixture should be vinylester as well. But this type of resin is not yet commonly used by the novice as an alternative product for blister repair.

10. When the last coat of resin is completely cured, wash the hull with water again to remove the amine blush.

11. Sand overall with 80-grit paper, wash the hull again, then read the instructions on the bottom-paint can to learn the recommended procedure for applying bottom paint.

✓ Once the hull has an epoxy barrier coat, it's important that it remain intact. One way to keep a watch on it is to paint the bottom with two layers of bottom paint, each a different color (for example, first coat red, second coat blue). During the course of normal boat use, when a spot of red shows, it's time to start thinking about repainting.

✓ In order to avoid an overzealous blasting of sand, the job can be done with baking soda, a less abrasive material.

Chapter 9

Stiffeners

This chapter describes typical problems relating to hull stiffening and shows the steps necessary to make repairs, but chapter 4 can also be referenced for details on working with the materials.

While the appearance of cracks and crazing on the gelcoat may not be a welcome sight, in one sense it could be regarded as a good thing—it provides early warning that the area around the cracks may need to be strengthened, and the sooner, the better.

Another indicator of weakness in a hull is the hint of an indentation at a critical stress area, such as the place where chain plates are fastened into a sailboat hull. Even more serious is the visible "oil-canning" effect that becomes noticeable when the boat moves through rough water. Among other problems, this hull flexing can lead to loose or detached bulkheads or stringers. Soft or spongy decks were mentioned in an earlier chapter, but not all soft decks are attributable to a core problem. Sometimes, the deck expanse simply does not have sufficient support below—it is too wide for the available stringers to provide solid support. Engine mounts frequently need attention because of the constantly changing pressures on them. Obviously, a boat has many areas that could benefit from stiffening. The suggestions in this chapter must necessarily be very general, but the methods of repair can be adapted to individual projects.

REINFORCING THE HULL

Just Add Fiberglass

Some sections of the hull can be strengthened by adding a few layers of fiberglass to the existing laminate, thus increasing the hull thickness.

1. Mark the area to be strengthened and clean the interior surface of all dirt, especially any oily spots.

2. With coarse sandpaper, grind/sand away the surface coating (paint and/or gelcoat) so the new fabric can be applied directly onto the existing fiberglass laminate.

3. Clear the surface of all sanding dust, wipe clean with appropriate cleaner.

4. Cut fiberglass fabric; each piece of fabric should be cut a bit smaller than the preceding piece, and lay-up should follow the large-to-small placement in order to avoid stress concentrations at the edge of the stiffened area.

5. Apply a coat of resin to the surface; place the first layer of fiberglass and add enough resin to saturate; continue with more plies to build up the desired thickness of the reinforcement. (If using epoxy, use a fast-curing hardener to combat epoxy's tendency to sag or drip down a vertical surface. For the same reason, a bit of colloidal silica can be added to the resin mix.)

6. After the last piece of fabric is in place, smooth out the surface with plain resin.

7. Finish the patch according to the usual methods for the type of resin being used.

Add a Stiffener

With this repair, a length of wood or other stiffener is fiberglassed onto the hull interior at areas that are prone to flexing. Because the strength of the repair will ultimately come from overlays of fiberglass cloth, the stiffener base can be a cardboard tube, halved lengthwise; the rounded surface accepts the fiberglass readily. If wood or foam core material is used, the edges should be beveled so

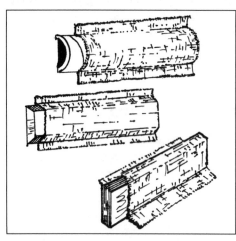

Make a stringer, using a cardboard tube or a piece of wood or foam core as the base. The strength will come from fiberglass laminated over the base.

Add a stiffener:
a. Tape the cardboard tube to the hull interior.

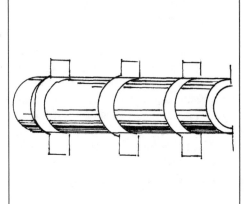

b. Apply thickened epoxy resin to make a fillet. When cured, remove the tape and finish the fillet.

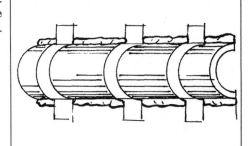

c. Laminate layers of fiberglass fabric over the tube and onto the surface on both sides.

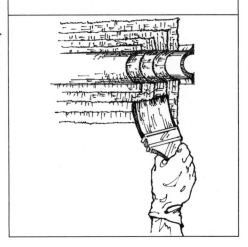

the fiberglass fabric will bond easily, with no sharp corners to resist bonding of the fabric.

1. Thoroughly clean the surface area where stiffener will be attached; be certain no oily residue remains.
2. Sand/grind the paint or gelcoat away, so the support piece will attach directly to the fiberglass laminate.
3. If using the cardboard half-tube, cut it to the desired length, and "glue" it in place with some thickened epoxy putty. Tape across it in a few spots to hold it tightly against the hull interior (or overhead), then mix more "peanut butter" putty and apply it at the seam where the tube meets the hull (between the tape pieces). Make a fillet with an ice cream stick or a spoon. When the putty cures, remove the tape and finish the fillet, sanding it to a smooth, even surface.
4. Cut pieces of fiberglass to fit over the tube and extend onto the hull surface. The first piece of fabric will be the largest; each of the remaining pieces will be narrower and shorter than the last, thus creating a graduated edge when the cloth is layered over the stiffener. The smallest piece of fabric will extend past the tube about 2 inches; the other pieces will step down to the hull surface in increments of ½ to ¾ inch.
5. Coat the tube with resin, then add the fiberglass cloth, saturating each piece in turn. The more fiberglass that is used over the stiffener, the stronger the support will be; four layers are probably enough for a typical application.
6. Finish by whatever method is compatible with the type of resin being used. Since these support pieces are usually located in places that aren't normally visible, they needn't be finished cosmetically at all.

✓ Epoxy is the best resin to use for this secondary bonding of added support pieces because of its strength and adhesive properties.

REINFORCING THE DECK

Even on a smaller boat, the foredeck area may be too wide for proper support by the existing stringers, causing the uncomfortable sensation of walking on a deck that seems to give with each step. Though it is not easy to add fiberglass on the underside of anything, it IS possible. Because "sag" is so critical in these applications (both sag time and literal resin sag), the quicker-drying finishing polyester resin has the advantage. Epoxy with fast hardener could also be used, and it has the advantage of being the stronger bonding material.

Fabric Patch Under Deck

The simplest fix is the laminated fabric patch, and it is certainly worth a try, as it would be the least messy fix. If it proves to be insufficient for the desired support, removal is not necessary—it can be the base for further stiffening.

1. Clean the overhead completely.
2. Grind/sand the surface to remove paint or gelcoat.
3. Cut fiberglass pieces. Because the fabric will tend to fall away from the overhead once it is heavy with resin, keep the size manageable—perhaps no larger than 11 by 14 inches. Because mat holds its "flatness" better than cloth, this is one area where its use might be an advantage, particularly for the first layer.
4. Mix the resin, adding a small amount of colloidal silica to lessen its tendency to drip. With a roller, coat the overhead with resin. Place the first piece of fiberglass, and use the roller to saturate it. Follow up with a grooved roller, to remove excess resin and encourage good adhesion. Watch the fabric as the resin cures; roll out any bubbles that appear and continue to push the fabric back onto the overhead if any sections pull away. With each piece of fabric, allow the resin to cure before adding more plies.

Stringers laminated under the foredeck can help support a wide expanse of deck.

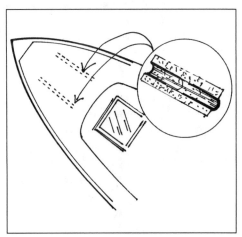

5. When the laminate has cured, sand any ragged areas and coat the patch with more resin to fair the edges into the existing surface. Finish the repair to blend with the surrounding area, though it is usually not necessary to completely fair the new patch into the overhead for a perfect match.

Tube Stringer Deck Support

Two cardboard tubes fiberglassed under the foredeck should improve the deck stiffness in this area. These stringers would be attached the same way as the one used for the hull reinforcement, except more care should be taken with the finished look, since these add-ons will probably be visible.

Plywood or Foam Panel Deck Support

The objective here is to bond plywood or foam panels to the overhead to really stiffen the deck. Because this project gets very messy, it is recommended that all movable items be taken out of the interior, including upholstered seat and back cushions. It will be necessary to brace the new panels against the overhead while the resin cures. The materials for bracing must be within easy reach to place them quickly once resin has been applied. A couple of lengths of 2 x 4 wedged between the cabin sole (or seat base) and the overhead will do the job.

1. Clean the overhead; sand/grind the surface coat on the section of overhead where the panel will be placed.
2. Cut the panel, keeping the size manageable (also about 11" x 14"). Bevel the edges of the panel so that when it is in place on the overhead, a covering layer of fiberglass fabric can turn over the edges and extend past the panel and onto the overhead. For each panel, cut one piece of fiberglass mat the same size, then cut at least two more pieces of fiberglass fabric larger than the panel to allow covering the edges and attaching to the overhead surface. (These pieces should also step down in application, each piece being slightly smaller than the preceding.)
3. When everything is ready, put on a pair of goggles and wear a hat or otherwise cover hair. Mix the resin. Roll a coat of resin on the overhead. Then saturate the piece of mat and place it on top of the panel. Hoist the panel up into place against the overhead (saturated mat will be between panel and overhead) and brace it tightly. Resin will likely ooze out all sides; be alert for drips.
4. Allow the resin to cure.

Plywood panel deck support: a. To prepare the surface for a stiffener panel, remove the gelcoat or other surface covering from the overhead.

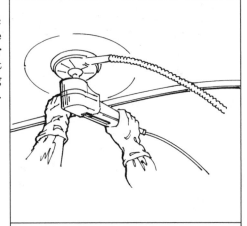

b. Put a piece of resin-saturated mat between the panel stiffener and the overhead. Brace the panel up with one or two lengths of 2 × 4 until the resin cures.

c. Use a roller to apply resin to cloth layers, which should cover the panel and extend onto the surface around the panel. (Bevel panel edges to allow fabric to turn over the edge.)

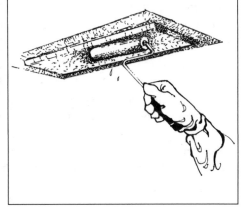

5. Remove the braces.
6. Sand away all rough places, add putty to all voids, and sand again. In general, smooth out the edges in preparation for the application of the fiberglass cloth.
7. Clean surface as necessary; roll on a coat of resin, put a piece of cloth in place and saturate it, turning the cloth over the edge of the panel and onto the overhead surface to extend beyond the panel by a couple of inches. Watch the fabric as it cures, using the grooved roller as necessary to push the cloth back against the surface if it starts to sag.
8. Add a second layer of fiberglass, more if desired. Then add more coats of resin to fill the fabric weave and leave a consistent texture. The panels can be finished smooth if desired, or the fabric or mat texture can be retained. Finish to blend with existing surface.

STRINGER REPAIR

A grid of support pieces runs under the sole of the boat. Made of wood or core material, these supports are tied into each other and into the hull or bulkheads with adhesive putty and more fiberglass. Filleting fills all joints, giving added support to the bond and providing the right surface for laminating layers of fiberglass. "Tabbing" (small pieces of fiberglass tape) further connects the grid.

Stringers are damaged in many ways. From inside, water soaks into wood and destroys it. From outside, a hard grounding or an impact with another object can force a separation. The constant pounding from normal use can shake something loose. Because stringers are the framework of the boat, it is critical that they be sound, so frequent inspections should be done to catch problems while they are still relatively easy to repair.

In every case, when damage is found, the repair should replicate original construction as closely as possible.

Damaged Stringer

If a stringer has some small areas of rot damage but is mainly intact, it may be possible to patch rather than replace the stringer.

1. Drill a grid of holes to establish the extent of the damage.
2. Dry the wood with a heat gun or hair dryer.
3. Use a syringe to inject thickened epoxy into the holes and into any voids between the wood stringer and the fiberglass skin.

4. When epoxy has cured, fair the surface and cover the stringer with a new layer of fiberglass fabric.

If the stringer shows extensive rot in one section only, it may be more practical to scarf in a new piece. Cut away the bad section and epoxy in a new one; bevel the ends where new and old meet so there is more surface to bond. Use epoxy putty at all joints and cover the repair with a layer of fiberglass cloth.

Destroyed Stringer

If the stringer is badly damaged, it should be replaced. Make note of its exact placement before removing it; take detailed measurements, since the actual markings will be removed in the process of cleaning the area for the new piece.

Using the old stringer (or a new pattern) for a template, cut the new stringer. Attach it to the substrate and to neighboring supports with epoxy putty; make fillets at all joints. Cover it with a few layers of fabric and additional resin. Tab it the same as the original. There is no need to finish it cosmetically.

✓ Biaxial tape is good for tabbing. The angled orientation of the fiber creates a stronger connection.

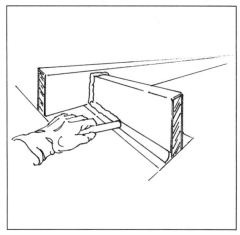

Replacement stringer:
a. Use epoxy putty to attach a replacement (or new) stringer and fillet all joints.

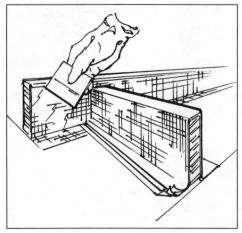

Replacement stringer:
b. Cover new stringers
with multiple layers of
fiberglass reinforcement.

Chapter 10

Other Applications

If a material can be versatile, then fiberglass is at the top of any list. The suggestions in this chapter are provided only as a starting point for an unending list of things that can be done with fiberglass materials and methods.

SMALL BOAT REPAIRS

If the dinghy, kayak, canoe, surfboard, or sailboard is indeed fiberglass, then the scratches and dings and nicks can all be repaired the same way as the big boats. Even aluminum canoes can take an emergency fiberglass patch.

✓ Emergency repairs can be made on-site if a tube of 5-minute epoxy is in the emergency kit. A patch of any kind of fabric can substitute for fiberglass.

✓ Patch a crack in the cowl of an outboard motor with resin and a piece of fabric applied to the inside. Starting with a clean surface may be the biggest challenge.

✓ Some small boats may look like fiberglass but they are actually made of other composites or molded compounds. While it may be possible to repair these items with fiberglass, they often require special preparation. Check with manufacturers.

AUTOMOTIVE REPAIRS

Muffler Patch

Anybody who ever bought a muffler- or tailpipe-fixing kit already has some experience with fiberglass repair, except that instead of woven fiberglass fabric, the patching material looks like screening, and both the screen and the putty product are made to be very heat-resistant. But the fixing aspect is easy: cover the hole with a piece of screen, overlapping the pipe enough to create a bond; cover the screen with some goo and let it set.

Epoxy-based products are also available to fix cracked fuel tanks, plastic tanks, and even "flexible" auto parts.

Body Work

Polyester-based products have long been the standard for car repairs. Many people first used polyester putty and fabric to patch a rusted fender or door panel, and many stories praise the power of Bondo. The procedure is much the same as for boat repair, except that with cars, the presence of rust adds another factor, a new kind of "clean" caution.

1. Clean the surface of all oil and dirt.
2. Sand all rusted areas until only bright metal is showing.
3. Fill small dents and holes with a thick putty; when that cures, sand again, and when surface is smooth, "paint" a coat of resin onto the steel. (If only surface defects were present, this may complete the patching portion of the repair. If, however, a section of metal is totally rusted away, a patch of fiberglass will be used to span the gap and create a new surface.)
4. Add layers of cloth and resin until the surface is solid. Smooth the surface with applications of putty, sanding between.
5. Sand the surface using fine-grit paper up to 600 wet/dry.
6. Spray paint using Preval Paint Sprayer (or a can of model-matched spray enamel).
7. Fine sand up to 1200, buff if necessary, and wax.

RECREATIONAL VEHICLES OF ALL KINDS

Motorhomes and travel trailers can be the objects of fiberglass repair, particularly the newer ones with the flat fiberglass siding. These units probably have as many opportunities for repair projects as boats, both outside and in. Dents or scratches and scrapes can be fixed the same way as they are on boats, except that the RVs don't require the high-gloss finish. Damaged corners can be totally rebuilt, even using a core material to help with the shaping, if so desired.

A small fix can halt what might become a big hassle. On many trailers, the screen door shows a common defect: from the inside, a small section of the door must slide open to allow access to the door handle. It is essential for this piece to slide closed again or the flying bugs find a welcome entry, but the sliding section is often broken.

A temporary fix of cardboard and duct tape creates an easy pattern. Someday, the fix can be made permanent using fiberglass materials.

On motorcycles, bicycles, snowmobiles, or ATVs, any number of small parts can be patched, strengthened, or fabricated using fiberglass, resin, and occasionally some ingenuity.

HOUSEHOLD APPLICATIONS

Concrete or Plaster Cracks

Cracks in the concrete floor of a basement or garage can be filled with an epoxy putty, sanded, and painted to be an acceptable match, not only repairing those cracks but hopefully discouraging the occurrence of more.

Cracks in a plaster wall or ceiling can be treated the same way. Open the crack more as with gelcoat scratches, fill with putty, sand, and finish.

Tile

Use thickened epoxy instead of mastic to set ceramic tiles on a wall or counter top. If the substrate is properly prepared, the epoxy will be a truly permanent base for the tiles. But use grout between the tiles, as usual.

Sink

Laundry-room sinks and basement washtubs are often made of fiberglass. Damaged corners or scrapes can be repaired easily with reinforced putty and perhaps some small pieces of fabric and resin. The truly ambitious worker could actually build a whole sink using fiberglass over a core material.

Use thick epoxy to attach the backsplash piece behind the kitchen sink.

Toilet Tank

Cracks or chips on the toilet tank can be fixed with epoxy. Dry the tank, epoxy the broken piece back in, and then cover the repair with a piece of fabric on the inside. Fill all gaps visible outside with more putty, and spot paint it when dry to match the glazed surface as closely as possible.

Door and Window Frames

Scarf in a piece of wood to replace a damaged or rotted section of door or window frame, using epoxy resin. A whole new window sill might someday be needed; coat it with a layer of cloth to prevent future water damage and rot.

On exterior wood trim, use epoxy to seal knots in place before painting.

Siding

Use resin to coat the bottom 6 or 8 inches of vertical "board and batten" wood siding before painting. This will discourage water from wicking up into the wood from the planting areas below. The same can be done to porch support poles and fence posts, though the damage in those locations would more likely come from water dripping from above than wicking from below.

Outdoor Furniture

Restore picnic tables or the favorite Adirondack chair. If necessary, patch individual planks from the underside with a piece of fabric or mat. Sand and coat all surfaces with resin before repainting to stop further checking or cracking.

Indoor Furniture

If a wooden tabletop or chair seat cracks, glue alone may not be strong enough for a permanent fix. Glue it first (using epoxy), and follow up with a layer or two of fiberglass fabric laminated to the underside of the table or chair. There's no need to finish the patch neatly—nobody will ever see it—but the cloth will give the needed support to make the repair permanent.

Picture Frames

Picture frames fall apart frequently. The mitered corners can be glued back together just as frequently, but if a small patch of fiberglass is bonded to the backside of each corner, repeat fixes will be unnecessary.

Hobby Use

Boat and airplane models can be built or repaired the same way as their full-size counterparts. Table setups for model trains can use fiberglass techniques for building everything from background mountains to buildings. Decorative tabletops are made with casting resin (another kind of liquid plastic), and thickened epoxy can glue almost anything, including jewelry fittings, dollhouse furniture, and musical instruments.

Glossary

AMINE BLUSH. A waxy coating that rises to the surface of epoxy resin as it cures.

ARAMID. Alternative to fiberglass reinforcement (Kevlar is one commonly recognized brand name).

BIAXIAL FABRIC. Two-layered fabric. Each layer consists of parallel strands of fiberglass stitched together; the two layers are then attached so the strands run at 45-degree angles to the edge of the fabric as it comes off the roll.

BIAXIAL FABRIC WITH MAT. A layer of mat stitched to biaxial fabric.

BLISTERS. Gelcoat "bubbles" filled with acidic fluid; may appear on boat hulls as a random few or an overall pattern.

BOAT POX. A description of the condition of a boat hull covered with hundreds of tiny blisters.

CARBON FIBER. Alternative to fiberglass reinforcement material; also referred to as graphite fiber.

CATALYST. The substance (MEKP) that prompts the cure of polyester resins.

CHALKED. Gelcoat or paint that is dull and has a faded appearance.

CHOPPED STRAND. Short pieces of fiberglass filament.

CHOPPER GUN. Used in the "chopped strand" method of fiberglass hull construction; resin and bits of fiberglass strands are simultaneously "shot" into the mold.

CLOSED-CELL FOAM. Core material that does not absorb water.

COLLOIDAL SILICA. Fine, powdery substance, used to thicken resin.

COMPOSITE. The buildup of layers of reinforcement fiber saturated with resin.

COSMETICS. Minor surface repairs.

CRAZING. Pattern of cracks in gelcoat, caused by impact or indicating an area under stress.

CURE. The change in resin from liquid to solid.

DEWAXER. Wax-removing solvent.

E-GLASS. Type of glass used for most boat construction and repair.

END-GRAIN BALSA. A core material made up of small squares of balsa wood held together by a thin fabric.

EPOXY RESIN. Type of resin often used for boat repair.

EXOTHERMIC REACTION. Heat produced during cure of resin.

FABMAT. Fiberglass fabric with mat attached.

FAIRING COMPOUND. Easy-to-sand thickened resin, used when smoothing large surface areas.

FIBERGLASS. Glass in the form of filaments; also, the fabric made from these filaments; also, the generic term used to describe resin/fabric composites, even if the fabric is NOT fiberglass.

FILLET. A rounded seam made with thickened resin to fill the joint where two parts meet.

FINISHING RESIN (SURFACING RESIN). Polyester resin used for final layer of construction; cures in air.

FRP. Fiber-reinforced plastic (often defined as fiberglass reinforced plastic).

GELCOAT. A type of polyester resin used for the finish coat.

GELCOAT PASTE. Thickened gelcoat used to patch small defects.

GRAPHITE. Carbon fiber.

GRP (GLASS-REINFORCED PLASTIC). The term used in England to describe fiberglass construction.

HAND LAY-UP. Plies of resin-saturated fiberglass fabric layered by hand into a mold to build the thickness of a boat hull.

HARDENER. Curing agent for epoxy resin.

HYDROLYSIS. The process by which fluid from osmotic blisters attacks the resin in the hull, leading to delamination and weakening of the structure.

ISOPHTHALIC RESIN. Type of polyester resin used in boat manufacture and repair in recent years. Less prone to blistering than earlier type.

KEVLAR. Trade name for aramid fabric.

KICK. Commonly used to describe the change in resin as it starts to cure.

LAMINATE. To build a thickness by bonding layers of resin-saturated fabric.

LAMINATING RESIN (LAY-UP RESIN). Polyester resin used for laminating; does not cure when exposed to air.

LAY-UP. Building hull thickness with plies of resin-saturated fiberglass fabric. Used to distinguish between a woven fabric composite and a chopped-strand composite.

MAT. Fiberglass fabric made of short strands of fiberglass filament, pressed together.

MATRIX. In fiberglass construction, resin is the matrix.

METHYL ETHYL KETONE PEROXIDE (MEKP). Catalyst used to cure polyester and vinylester resin.

MICROBALLOONS, MICROSPHERES. Tiny, hollow phenolic spheres used to thicken resin.

MILLED GLASS FIBERS. Small bits of fiberglass fabric, used to thicken resin.

NONSKID. Granules mixed into paint to prevent a slick surface on decks. Also, that section of deck that has the nonskid treatment.

OIL-CANNING. Visible flexing of a boat hull. Indicates area that needs to be strengthened.

ORANGE-PEEL. Wrinkled surface that may appear in spots after a new coat of paint dries; indicates the paint coating was too thick when applied.

ORTHOPHTHALIC RESIN. Type of polyester resin initially used in the manufacture of fiberglass boats.

OSMOSIS. The process by which water is brought into gelcoat voids; the resulting problem is sometimes referred to as osmotic blistering.

OXIDATION. Deterioration of gelcoat; surface appears faded and chalky.

PIGMENT. Resin coloring agent.

POLISHING COMPOUND. Wax-like product used for final finishing of gelcoat and some paints.

POLYESTER RESIN. Resin commonly used in boat construction and many repairs.

POLYVINYL ALCOHOL (PVA). Keeps air away from gelcoat, allowing gelcoat to cure.

POT LIFE. The amount of time resin will stay liquid in the container after mixing.

PRIMARY BONDING. All plies in a laminate are bonded chemically through the initial thermosetting process.

PRINT-THROUGH. Pattern of fiberglass cloth showing through gelcoat, sometimes long after initial construction.

REINFORCEMENT. The fiber, or fabric, component of a composite.

RELEASE FABRIC. A material that can be placed over wet resin to smooth out a repair area; will not adhere to cured resin.

RESIN. Liquid plastic; may be polyester, vinylester, or epoxy.

RESIN-INFUSION MOLDING. A variation of vacuum-bag molding that introduces resin after vacuum is applied.

RUBBING COMPOUND. Wax-like product for final finishing of gelcoat.

SANDWICH CONSTRUCTION. A type of construction that places a core material between outer skins of fiberglass.

SECONDARY BONDING. Mechanical or adhesive bonding of repairs.

S-GLASS. Structural grade of glass with very high tensile strength; not usually used in boat repair.

SPIDER CRACKS. A common, spider-web pattern of cracks on gelcoat, caused by impact or indicating an area of stress.

SPONGY DECK. Deck section that feels soft underfoot; usually indicates problem with core.

SPRAY-UP. Another term for "chopper-gun" construction.

SPREADER. Thin, rectangular-shaped plastic with beveled edge; used to spread resin over cloth, or to spread thickened putty into scratches and dents.

SQUEEGEE. Spreader.

STRINGER. Structural support beam inside hull.

STYRENE. Sometimes used as thinner or cleaner for polyester resins.

TAPE. Fiberglass fabric in narrow widths.

THERMOSETTING RESIN. Resin that cures with heat generated by catalyst or hardener.

THIXOTROPIC. Consistency of thickened resin; prevents resin from sagging.

TRIAXIAL FABRIC. Three-layered fabric, with each layer made up of parallel strands of fiberglass. Layers are placed so filaments run at different angles to each other.

UNIDIRECTIONAL FABRIC. Fabric made of parallel strands of fiberglass stitched together.

VACUUM-BAG MOLDING. Process that removes trapped air from a mold after the fabric has been saturated with resin, ensuring complete adhesion and absence of voids between fabric plies.

VINYLESTER RESIN. A type of polyester resin.

WET OUT. To saturate fiberglass cloth with resin.

WOVEN FABRIC. A cross weave of fiberglass filaments woven like ordinary cloth, with fiber rows running at 90 degrees to each other.

WOVEN ROVING. Heavy-weight fiberglass fabric made of large strands of glass.

Problems

A high percentage of the problems experienced when working with resins fall under a very basic umbrella: incorrect ratio of resin to catalyst/hardener and/or incomplete mixing of the two.

When measuring MEKP for polyester resin, it is easy to miscount drops, or squeeze the container (whether tube or eyedropper) too much so the drops become a continuous flow, which is impossible to measure.

With epoxy, a person could mistakenly measure the wrong combination: is the desired ratio 2:1, 3:1, or 5:1? In addition, if using pumps to dispense resin and hardener, the pumps may need to be checked—especially after being stored for a time—to confirm that they are dispensing the proper amount of resin and hardener.

Any resin must be mixed uniformly; one minute mixing time is the minimum recommended, scraping the container sides often, and a little extra time is just extra insurance.

Thickeners and pigments should be added after the resin and catalyst/hardener have been mixed.

POLYESTER RESIN

Problem:

Resin starts to cure too fast; it gels or turns lumpy in the mixing container.

Cause: Too much MEKP; very high outside temperature; resin stayed in the container too long.

Solution: Throw away any resin that starts to gel (set it aside until it solidifies). Next time, use less MEKP; work in cooler part of day when possible; be sure to mix resin thoroughly; use a larger mixing container so the level of resin is shallower. (Too much catalyst will make the composite brittle.)

Problem:
Resin does not cure solid, but remains sticky.

Cause: Laminating resin was used in error. Resin and catalyst were not mixed thoroughly. Wrong mix ratio.

Solution: If laminating resin was used in error, simply recoat with finishing resin. If the uncured resin IS finishing resin, remove it (scrape with putty knife or paint scraper, then wash the surface thoroughly with acetone or lacquer thinner) and apply a new coat.

Problem:
Gelcoat does not cure.

Cause: Incorrect mix ratio. Excessive humidity. Cold temperature. PVA or plastic covering did not seal out air completely.

Solution: Apply heat with heat gun or heat lamp. If gelcoat still remains tacky after a day of heat application, remove the gelcoat and apply a new coat. If possible, wait for ideal weather conditions to reapply, and do the work early enough in the day to avoid late afternoon dampness. Measure carefully, mix thoroughly. Be sure surface is clean and gelcoat is completely sealed from air.

Alternately, use "finishing gelcoat," which includes an air-blocking substance for self-curing (like finishing resin).

Problem:
Stored resin is starting to thicken or gel.

Cause: If polyester resin is stored in a warm place, or in a translucent container, or in a half-empty can, it may cure even without the addition of catalyst.

Solution: Store resin in a dark, cool place; pour leftover resin into smaller containers to minimize air space in the can.

EPOXY RESIN
Problem:
Resin starts to cure sooner than expected. Mixing container gets warm, resin may start to smoke.

Cause: High outside temperature. Wrong hardener or incorrect mixing ratio. Too much resin confined in mixing container for too long a time.

Solution: Move container away from work area and allow the epoxy to cure completely before disposing of it. If necessary, scrape any lumpy cured epoxy off repair area; sand and clean surface to prepare for new resin. Use correct hardener for the temperature. Use a larger mixing container so resin will be shallower, with more surface exposed (the more confined the resin, the faster it will cure).

Problem:

Newly applied coat of resin shows spots—a few isolated spots or a whole section of them—where resin seems to be shrinking away from the surface.

Cause: Contamination on the surface (could be water, dirty solvent, oil, fingerprints, etc.)

Solution: Remove the coat of epoxy; scrape and wash the surface with lacquer thinner or alcohol. When dry, sand and clean thoroughly to ensure adhesion for new epoxy coating.

Problem:

Tiny bubbles appear on surface of epoxy soon after application.

Cause: Pockets of air in the resin rise to the surface as the temperature increases (combination of warm outside temperature and the heat produced in the curing process). Worse when the epoxy is applied in too thick a coat.

Solution: While epoxy is still liquid, use a foam brush and lightly brush over the bubbles to break them.

Problem:

Resin does not cure in the expected time frame. Sticky to touch.

Cause: Improper mix ratio. Incomplete mixing. Cool temperature.

Solution: Apply heat with a heat gun or heat lamp. If resin still does not cure, use a scraper to remove as much resin as possible, then clean off the rest with alcohol or lacquer thinner. (The heat gun can be used to further soften the uncured epoxy so it will be easier to scrape off.)

When ready to reapply, measure resin/hardener ratio carefully and mix thoroughly. Check pumps to be sure they are providing accurate measures. If temperature is still cool, warm the resin before application (place resin container in a bucket of warm water), and/or choose the hardener made for use in low temperature.

Note: It is sometimes suggested that a new coat of epoxy can be applied over the uncured coat, and eventually, all will cure. Personal experience with this "shortcut" resulted in a section of deck where the new epoxy coat cured perfectly, then peeled away perfectly from the underlayer of still-rubbery resin.

Problem

Cured epoxy is covered with a waxy film that clogs sandpaper.

Cause: Not a problem, this is to be expected; amine blush rises to the surface of epoxy during curing. Once the epoxy has cured, the blush must be removed before overcoating with additional coats of epoxy or with paint primer.

Solution: Remove the blush by wet sanding or washing with water and a scrub pad. (If a release fabric was used in the resin application, the blush will be removed along with the release fabric.)

Problem:

Surface of epoxy appears milky, all over or in random spots.

Cause: Resin was applied too late in the day and condensation affected cure time. The boat is in an area of high humidity.

Solution: Most likely, the epoxy will cure completely once all the moisture dries out. If the day is cloudy or the boat is in an area of high humidity, use a heat lamp or heat gun to hurry the drying process.

Problem:

Runs or drips appear in the epoxy on vertical surfaces.

Cause: No thickening (sag-prevention) agent was added to the resin. Resin was applied in too heavy a coating.

Solution: Sand the lumpy surface. Thicken resin slightly with colloidal silica so resin resists sagging and roll on new, thin coats.

Problem:

A section of fabric lifted away from the surface as resin cured, leaving a large void beneath.

Cause: Too much resin caused fabric to float off the surface. Surface was not properly prepared (amine blush not removed; surface of cured epoxy not cleaned or sanded).

Solution: Try removing the raised portion (cut it away with a mat knife and sand the edges). If the surrounding area seems sound, place a new piece of cloth into the cutaway portion. However, if cloth continues to lift at edges as you sand, remove the whole piece. Use a heat gun to soften the cured epoxy. With one hand, scrape underneath the cloth with a putty knife; with the other hand, pull the fabric away from the surface.

Sand and clean thoroughly before applying new fabric layer.

Problem:

After storage, hardener turns dark reddish-brown.

Cause: A normal occurrence. Probably OK to use for general repairs (naturally excluding clear-coat application).

Solution: Before using it for a repair project, mix a small amount of resin and test it to be sure it cures properly.

Index

*More boating books from
Cornell Maritime Press and
Tidewater Publishers*

Advanced First Aid Afloat
    Peter F. Eastman, M.D.; John M. Levinson, M.D., Editor
    ISBN 10: 0-87033-524-3   ISBN 13: 978-0-87033-524-2

Boater's Medical Companion
    Robert S. Gould, M.D.
    ISBN 10: 0-87033-402-6   ISBN 13: 978-0-87033-402-3

Boater's Weather Guide
    Margaret Williams
    ISBN 10: 0-87033-417-4   ISBN 13: 978-0-87033-417-7

Celestial for the Cruising Navigator
    Merle B. Turner
    ISBN 10: 0-87033-341-0   ISBN 13: 978-0-87033-341-5

Celestial Navigation
    Frances W. Wright
    ISBN 10: 0-87033-291-0   ISBN 13: 978-0-87033-291-3

Celestial Navigation by H O 249
    John E. Milligan
    ISBN 10: 0-87033-191-4   ISBN 13: 978-0-87033-191-6

Complete Book of Anchoring and Mooring
    Earl R. Hinz
    ISBN 10: 0-87033-539-1   ISBN 13: 978-0-87033-539-6

Cornell Manual, The
    John M. Keever
    ISBN 10: 0-87033-559-6   ISBN 13: 978-0-87033-559-4

Diesel Engines
    Leo Block, P.E.
    ISBN 10: 0-87033-418-2   ISBN 13: 978-0-87033-418-4

Dockmanship
David Owen Bell
ISBN 10: 0-87033-425-5 ISBN 13: 978-0-87033-425-2

Encyclopedia of Knots and Fancy Rope Work
Raoul Graumont and John Hensel
ISBN 10: 0-87033-021-7 ISBN 13: 978-0-87033-021-6

Essential Seamanship
Richard Henderson
ISBN 10: 0-87033-456-5 ISBN 13: 978-0-87033-456-6

Fisherman's Knots and Nets
Raoul Graumont and Elmer Wenstrom
ISBN 10: 0-87033-024-1 ISBN 13: 978-0-87033-024-7

Handbook of Knots
Raoul Graumont
ISBN 10: 0-87033-030-6 ISBN 13: 978-0-87033-030-8

How to Avoid Huge Ships
John W. Trimmer
ISBN 10: 0-87033-433-6 ISBN 13: 978-0-87033-433-7

How to Navigate Today
Leonard Gray
ISBN 10: 0-87033-353-4 ISBN 13: 978-0-87033-353-8

Learn to Navigate
Charles A. Whitney and Frances W. Wright
ISBN 10: 0-87033-426-3 ISBN 13: 978-0-87033-426-9

Nautical Etiquette and Customs
Lindsay Lord
ISBN 10: 0-87033-356-9 ISBN 13: 978-0-87033-356-9

Nautical Rules of the Road
B. A. Farnsworth and Larry C. Young
ISBN 10: 0-87033-408-5 ISBN 13: 978-0-87033-408-5

A Star to Steer Her By
Edward J. Bergin
ISBN 10: 0-87033-309-7 ISBN 13: 978-0-87033-309-5